OF WATER AND THE SPIRIT

OF WATER AND THE SPIRIT

A LITURGICAL STUDY OF BAPTISM

by

Alexander Schmemann

Professor of Liturgical Theology
St. Vladimir's Seminary

ST. VLADIMIR'S SEMINARY PRESS
1974

by the same author

FOR THE LIFE OF THE WORLD: SACRAMENTS AND ORTHODOXY (1963)

THE HISTORICAL ROAD OF EASTERN ORTHODOXY (1963)

ULTIMATE QUESTIONS: AN ANTHOLOGY OF RUSSIAN RELIGIOUS THOUGHT (1965)

INTRODUCTION TO LITURGICAL THEOLOGY (1966)

GREAT LENT (1969)

Library of Congress Cataloging in Publication Data:
Schmemann, Alexander, 1921-
    Of water and the spirit.
    Bibliography: p. 155
    1. Baptism—Orthodox Eastern Church. I. Title.
BX378.B3S35   234'.161   74-30061

ISBN 0-913836-10-9

© Copyright 1974

St. Vladimir's Seminary Press

First Printing 1974
Second Printing 1983

PRINTED IN THE UNITED STATES OF AMERICA
BY
ATHENS PRINTING COMPANY

Contents

INTRODUCTION

To Rediscover Baptism

1.

In the past, during the "golden age" of Christian liturgy, the sacrament of Baptism was performed on the paschal night as an organic part of the great annual celebration of Easter.[1] Even today, long after the link between the two solemnities has been broken, the baptismal rites and the paschal liturgy still keep an indelible mark of their initial connection and interdependence.[2] Not many Christians, however, are aware of this. Not many know that the liturgy of Easter is primarily a baptismal liturgy; that when on Easter eve they hear the biblical readings about the crossing of the Red Sea, or the three children in the furnace, or Jonah in the whale's womb, they listen to the most ancient "paradigms" of Baptism and attend the great baptismal vigil. They do not know that the joy which illumines the holy night, when the glorious announcement "Christ is Risen!" resounds, is the joy of those who were "baptized into Christ and have put on Christ," who were "buried with Him by baptism into death that like as Christ was raised up from the dead by the glory of the Father," even so they also should walk in the "newness of life" (Rom. 6:4). Not many Christians have been taught that Easter as a liturgical feast, and Lent as a liturgical preparation for Easter, developed originally from the celebration of Baptism; that Pascha, the "Feast of Feasts," is thus truly the fulfillment of Baptism, and Baptism is truly a paschal sacrament.

Knowing all this, however, is more than just learning an interesting chapter in liturgical archeology. It is indeed the only way to a fuller understanding of Baptism, of its meaning in the life of the Church and in our individual lives as Christians. And it is this fuller understanding of the fundamental mystery of the Christian faith and Christian life that, more than anything else, we badly need today.

Why? Because, to put it very simply, Baptism is *absent* from our life. It is, to be sure, still accepted by all as a self-evident necessity. It is not opposed, not even questioned. It is performed all the time in our churches. It is, in other terms, "taken for granted." Yet, in spite of all this, I dare to affirm that in a very real sense it is absent, and this "absence" is at the root of many tragedies of the Church today.

Baptism is, first of all, absent from the Church's *liturgy,* if by liturgy we mean that which the term *leitourgia* has always meant: a corporate act in which the whole Church, i.e. the entire community, is involved, in which it really participates. Is it not true indeed that, from the liturgical point of view, Baptism today has become a private family celebration performed as a rule outside the corporate worship of the Church, precisely outside its *leitourgia?* Is it not true that one can be a regular church-goer for years and years without having attended one Baptism, without even knowing how it is performed?

Being thus absent from liturgy, Baptism then is naturally absent from our *piety.* A Christian of the past knew, for example, that Easter each year was the celebration of his own Baptism, of his own entrance into and participation in the life of the Risen Christ. He knew that the Resurrection of Christ was again revealed and reaffirmed in this act of regeneration and rebirth through which new members were integrated into the "newness of life." But today's Christian does not relate either himself or the Church to Baptism. He knows, of course, that he was baptized and that Baptism is a necessary condition for his membership in the Church. But this knowledge remains abstract. It is not referred to the Church as the very community of those who died with Christ and who therefore were given a new life in Him. His piety is thus no longer baptismal, as was that of the early Christians. Baptism for him has ceased to be a permanent reality and experience illuminating his whole life, an ever-living source of joy and hope. It is recorded somewhere on a baptismal certificate but certainly not in his Christian memory. And he no longer experiences Easter and Pentecost, Christmas and Epiphany, and indeed the whole liturgy of the Church, in their direct relationship to Baptism, as realities whose meaning and efficacy in the Church are fulfilled in and through Baptism.

Finally, having ceased to feed Christian piety, Baptism obviously has lost its power to shape our Christian worldview, i.e. our basic attitudes, motivations and decisions. There exists today no Christian "philosophy of life" which would embrace the totality of our existence, family as well as profession, history as well as society, ethics as well as action. There is simply no difference between the "values" and "ideals" accepted inside the Christian community and those accepted outside of it. A Christian today may be a "parishioner in good standing" while living by standards and philosophies of life having nothing to do with, if not openly opposed to, the Christian faith.

A Christian of the past knew not only intellectually but with his entire being that through Baptism he was placed into a radically new relationship with all aspects of life and with the "world" itself; that he received, along with his faith, a radically new understanding of life. Baptism for him was the starting point and also the foundation of a Christian "philosophy of life," of a permanent sense of direction guiding him firmly throughout his entire existence, supplying answers to all questions, solving all problems.

This foundation is still here with us. Baptism is performed. But it has ceased to be comprehended as the door leading into a new life and as the power to fight for this new life's preservation and growth in us.

2.

Such is the tragic consequence of what to many may seem a secondary and purely external development: the transformation of Baptism into a private ceremony, its ceasing to be the very heart of the Church's liturgy and piety. From a purely formal—dogmatical or canonical—point of view, this may seem unimportant. Is not Baptism valid regardless of how many people attend, of the time and place of its celebration, of the quantity of water used? Yet the very existence of such a "point of view" reveals how deeply divorced from the true spirit and tradition of the Church is our modern dogmatical and canonical consciousness, how radically ignorant it is of the old principle *lex orandi lex est credendi,* "the norm of prayer is the norm of belief."

The simple fact is that such a "point of view," taught today as an Orthodox norm, is the result of that "Western pseudomorphosis" of Orthodox theology which began after the patristic age came to its end and which poisoned the Church with a legalistic spirit totally alien to the Fathers and the early Tradition. This Western influence resulted in a narrowing of the very understanding of Baptism. Indeed one can read and reread contemporary manuals of Orthodox theology without ever finding out *why* water is used in Baptism, what is its connection with Christ's Death and Resurrection, why the Holy Chrism is to be consecrated by bishops alone—explanations obviously essential for the understanding of the baptismal mystery. In these manuals Baptism is defined almost exclusively as being the "removal" of original sin and as the conferring of grace, both acts being "necessary," in a juridical sense of this word, for salvation.[3] But Baptism as the sacrament of regeneration, as re-creation, as the personal Pascha and the personal Pentecost of man, as the integration into the *laos,* the people of God, as the "passage" from an old into a new life and finally as an epiphany of the Kingdom of God: all these meanings which made Baptism so central and so essential to early Christian piety and experience are virtually ignored, and this precisely because they do not fit into the legalistic framework adopted from the West.

This type of theology has said virtually everything about the *validity* of sacraments in general and of Baptism in particular. The only question which does not seem to be of interest to it is: *what* is being made valid in Baptism? And for this reason this official theology has in fact helped and accelerated the liturgical decadence which little by little chased Baptism from the *leitourgia* of the Church and made it into a private ceremony. If the "validity" of the sacrament requires nothing but a valid priest and a minimum of water, if, furthermore, nothing but "validity" is important, why not reduce the sacrament to these essential prerequisites? Why not have water and oil blessed in advance in order to save our precious time? Why bother with archaic rubrics which prescribe that "all the candles be lighted" and the priest "be vested in white vestments"? Why involve the parish, the congregation, the people of God in all this? Thus today it takes some fifteen minutes to perform in a dark corner of a church, with one "psaltist" giving the responses, an act in which the Fathers saw and acclaimed the greatest solemnity of the Church: a mystery "which fills with joy the angels and the archangels and all the powers from above and the earthly creatures," a mystery for which the Church prepared herself by forty days of fasting and which constituted the very essence of her paschal joy. A decadent liturgy supported by a decadent theology and leading to a decadent piety: such is the sad situation in which we find ourselves today and which must be corrected if we love the Church and want her to become again the power which transforms the life of man.

3.

We must rediscover Baptism—its meaning, its power, its true *validity*. The purpose of this essay is to help in such

a rediscovery, or rather to enumerate preliminary conditions
for it. For the real rediscovery must take place each time
the Church celebrates this great mystery and makes all of us
its participants and witnesses.

The goal of liturgical theology, as its very name indicates,
is to overcome the fateful divorce between theology, liturgy
and piety—a divorce which, as we have already tried to show
elsewhere,[4] has had disastrous consequences for theology as
well as for liturgy and piety. It deprived liturgy of its proper
understanding by the people, who began to see in it beautiful
and mysterious ceremonies in which, while attending them,
they take no real part. It deprived theology of its living source
and made it into an intellectual exercise for intellectuals. It
deprived piety of its living content and term of reference.
But it was not so with the Fathers. If their theology is still
for us the criterion and the source of inspiration, it is because
it is rooted in the living experience of the Church, in the great
reality of the worshipping community. It is indeed quite
revealing that the theological explanation of Baptism originated as a catechetical explanation of the baptismal rites—
as, in fact, an organic part of the liturgy itself. Theology
here began as an inspired reflection on the liturgy, as the
revelation of its true meaning. And when we read the Fathers,
how refreshingly far we are from the superficial symbolical
explanations of the liturgical rites so typical of the post-
patristic literature, how far also from the cold legalistic
definitions of our manuals!

To understand liturgy from inside, to discover and experience that "epiphany" of God, world and life which the
liturgy contains and communicates, to relate this vision and
this power to our own existence, to all our problems: such
is the purpose of liturgical theology. Of all this, Baptism
is truly the beginning, the foundation, and the key. The
whole life of the Church is rooted in the New Life which
shone forth from the grave on the first day of the new
creation. It is this new life that is given in Baptism and is
fulfilled in the Church. We began this introduction with the
mention of the initial liturgical connection between Pascha
and Baptism. This whole study is indeed nothing else but an

attempt to explain the meaning of this connection and to communicate, inasmuch as it is possible for our poor human words, the joy with which it fills our Christian life.

CHAPTER I

Preparation for Baptism

1. The Meaning of Preparation

For several centuries now the Church has been practicing almost exclusively *infant Baptism.* It is all the more significant, then, that liturgically the sacrament has nevertheless preserved the form and the structure it had when the majority of those baptized were adults. This is especially evident in the preparatory rites which in our present liturgical books are grouped under the heading: *The Prayers at the Reception of Catechumens.*[1]

This office, relatively short today, is the last surviving element of a long preparation for Baptism—preparation which in the past, and depending on the various local traditions, lasted from one to three years. The candidates for Baptism, called *catechumens,* were progressively introduced into the life of the Church by special rites which included exorcisms, prayers, explanations of the Holy Scripture, etc. This preparation involved the entire community, which thus was preparing itself for the reception of the new members. And it is from this double preparation—that of the catechumen and that of the Church—that there developed the pre-

paschal liturgical season which today we call Great Lent.[2]
It was the time of the ultimate and intensive preparation
for the "holy night," whose climax was precisely the "illumination" of those coming to Christ and seeking salvation
and new life in Him.

What is the meaning of this preparation? The question
is important because the predominance today of infant
Baptism seems to make some of these preparatory rites
irrelevant anachronisms. But the obvious importance they
had for the early Church and still have in liturgical tradition,
and the preservation by the Church of the "adult" structure
of Baptism, clearly indicate that in the eyes of the Church
this preparation is an integral part of the baptismal liturgy.
It is, then, by answering this question that we must begin
our explanation of Baptism.

We must realize first of all that preparation is a constant
and essential aspect of the Church's worship as a whole. It
is impossible to enter into the spirit of liturgy, to understand
its meaning and truly to participate in it without first understanding that it is built primarily on the double rhythm of
preparation and *fulfillment,* and that this rhythm is essential
to the Church's liturgy because it reveals and indeed fulfills
the double nature and function of the Church herself.[3]

On the one hand the Church herself *is* preparation: she
"prepares" us for life eternal. Thus her function is to transform our whole life into preparation. By her preaching,
doctrine and prayer she constantly reveals to us that the
ultimate "value" which gives meaning and direction to our
lives is at the "end," is "to come," is to be hoped for,
expected, anticipated. And without this basic dimension of
"preparation" there simply is no Christianity and no Church.
Thus the liturgy of the Church is always and primarily a
preparation: it always points and tends beyond itself, beyond
the present, and its function is to make us enter into that
preparation and thus to transform our life by referring it to
its fulfillment in the Kingdom of God.

Yet, on the other hand, the Church is also and essentially
fulfillment. The events which gave her birth and which
constitute the very source of her faith and life have taken

place. Christ has come. In Him man was deified and has ascended to heaven. The Holy Spirit has come and His coming has inaugurated the Kingdom of God. Grace has been given and the Church truly is "heaven on earth," for in her we have access to Christ's table in His Kingdom. We have received the Holy Spirit and can partake, here and now, of the new life and be in communion with God.

It is in and through liturgy that this double nature of the Church is revealed and communicated to us. It is the proper function of the liturgy to "make" the Church preparation and to reveal her as fulfillment. Every day, every week, every year is thus transformed and made into this double reality, into a correlation between the "already" and the "not yet." We could not have prepared ourselves for the Kingdom of God which is "yet to come" if the Kingdom were not "already" given to us. We could never have made the *end* an object of love, hope and desire if it were not revealed to us as a glorious and radiant *beginning*. We could never have prayed "Thy Kingdom come!" if we did not have the taste of that Kingdom already communicated to us. If the liturgy of the Church would not have been "fulfillment," our life could never have become "preparation." Thus this double rhythm of preparation and fulfillment, far from being accidental, constitutes the very essence of the liturgical life of the Church, of the liturgy not only in its totality but also in each of its component parts—each season, each service, each sacrament. What would Pascha be without the white quiet of the Holy and Blessed Sabbath? The solemn darkness of Good Friday without the long Lenten preparation? Yet, is not the sadness of Lent made into a "bright sadness" by the light which comes to it from the Pascha it prepares? If today the liturgy of the Church has ceased to be for so many people the deepest need and joy of their life, it is, above all, because they have forgotten, or maybe have never known, the essential liturgical law of preparation and fulfillment. They experience no fulfillment because they ignore preparation, and they ignore preparation because they desire no fulfillment. Then indeed liturgy appears as an irrelevant survival of archaic forms, to be enlivened by some "concert" or artificial and tasteless "solemnity."

Baptism is no exception to this fundamental principle. It requires preparation even if the human being to be baptized is only a few days old and is unable to understand that which will happen to him. The Orthodox Church, radically different in this from some "rationalistic" sects, has never posited "understanding" as the condition for Baptism. She would rather say that true "understanding" is made possible by Baptism, is its result and fruit, rather than its condition. We are very far from the flat idea that Baptism cannot be received unless it is "understood" and "accepted," and therefore is to be given only to "adults." Maybe the ultimate grace of Baptism is indeed that it makes us children, restores in us that "childhood" without which, in the words of Christ Himself, it is impossible to receive the Kingdom of God. What preparation means therefore is a total act of the Church, the recapitulation by her of all that makes baptismal regeneration possible. For the whole Church is changed, enriched and fulfilled when another child of God is integrated into her life and becomes a member of Christ's Body.

Baptism, we said, is a paschal sacrament, and Pascha means "passage," "pass-over." This passage begins in the preparatory rites and makes them the true beginning of the sacrament, the preparation for that which will find its fulfillment in the mystery of Water and the Spirit.

2. The Catechumenate

The *Prayers at the Reception of Catechumens* are preceded by the following rubric:

The priest loosens the girdle of the person who desires Illumination and removes it, and puts it off from him; and places him with his face toward the east, clothed in one garment only, unshod, and with head uncovered, and with his arms hanging by his sides; and he breathes thrice in his face; and signs his brow and his breast thrice with the sign of the cross; and lays his hand upon his head...

This rubric needs to be explained, and the rites it describes must be placed in the context of the entire pre-baptismal preparation.

In the early Church the one who desired to become a Christian was brought to the bishop of the local church by his *sponsors*,[4] i.e. those members of the Christian community who could testify to the serious intentions of the candidate, to the genuine character of his *conversion*. The conversion itself is, of course, beyond all explanations. What brings a man to Christ? What makes him believe? In spite of all attempts to classify and to describe various "types" of conversions, there always remains the mystery of the unique relationship between God and each human person whom God created for Himself. Our explanation begins therefore at the moment when this mysterious process has resulted in an objective decision: *to seek Baptism, to enter the Church.*

The convert was brought to the bishop, who in the early Church was the priest, the pastor and the teacher of the local Christian community. Having been assured of the seriousness of the convert's intentions, the bishop inscribed his name on the register of the catechumens.[5] Then he made three signs of the cross on the catechumen's face and laid his hand upon the catechumen's head. These first rites, called *enrollment*, signify that Christ takes possession of this person, inscribes him in the "book of life." At the time of St. John Chrysostom, this "enrollment" took place at the very beginning of Lent.[6] Today it constitutes the initial step of the baptismal liturgy itself, and we find its meaning expressed in the first prayer "at the reception of the catechumen."

> In Thy Name, O Lord God of Truth, and in the name of Thine Only-Begotten Son, and of Thy Holy Spirit, *I lay my hand* upon Thy servant who has been found worthy to flee unto Thy Holy Name and to take refuge under the shelter of Thy wings. Remove far from him his former delusion, and fill him with the faith, hope and love which are in Thee; that he may know that Thou art the only true God with Thine Only-Begotten Son, our Lord Jesus Christ, and Thy Holy Spirit. Enable him to walk in all Thy commandments, and to fulfill those things which are well pleasing unto Thee; for if a man do these things, he shall find life in them. *Inscribe him in Thy Book of Life,* and unite him to the flock of Thine inheritance. And may Thy Holy Name be glorified in him, together with that of Thy beloved Son, our Lord Jesus Christ, and of Thy life-giving Spirit. Let Thine eyes ever regard him with

mercy, and let Thine ears attend unto the voice of his supplication.
Make him to rejoice in the works of his hands, and in all his
generation; that he may render praise unto Thee, may sing, worship
and glorify Thy great and exalted Name always, all the days of his
life; for all the powers of Heaven sing praises unto Thee, and
Thine is the glory of the Father, and the Son, and of the Holy
Spirit, now and ever, and unto the ages of ages, Amen.

Thus, in this very first prayer, at the very beginning of
the baptismal liturgy, we are given the real dimensions,
the true content of conversion. Above all it is *fleeing* from
"this world" which has been stolen from God by the Enemy
and has become a prison. Conversion is not an event in the
realm and on the level of ideas, as so many people think
today. It is not the choice of an "ideology," not even an
answer to "problems"—a word delightfully ignored by the
early Church and the Holy Scripture. It is truly an escape from
darkness and despair. One comes to Christ in order to be
saved and because there is no other salvation. And the first
act of the baptismal liturgy is an act of protection: the bishop's
hand—the hand of Christ Himself—protects, shelters, "covers
with wings. . . ." For it is a mortal fight that is about to begin
now, and it is about its ultimate seriousness that we hear
in this first prayer.

The catechumen is now "enrolled," inscribed in the Book
of Life, and will soon be "united to the flock of God's
inheritance." At the same time he is also informed of the
ultimate goal of Baptism: the restoration of *true life,* the life
that man has lost in sin. This life is described as "rendering
praise, singing, worshiping and glorifying the great and
exalted Name." But this is a description of "heaven" and of
"eternity"; this is what, according to the Scriptures, the
heavenly powers eternally do before the Throne of God.
Salvation, restoration of life, the gift of life eternal: such
are the dimensions of Baptism as revealed in this first step
of the baptismal liturgy. The decisive event has begun.

3.   Exorcisms

The preparation for Baptism or "catechumenate" included

instructions and *exorcisms.*[7] Since today, because of infant Baptism, instruction in the faith has of necessity been relegated to the time after Baptism, we shall first speak of exorcisms, which in our present baptismal rite immediately follow the "prayer at the reception."

The "modern man," even an Orthodox, is usually quite surprised when he learns that the baptismal liturgy begins with words addressed to the Devil. The Devil indeed has no place in his religious outlook; he belongs to the panoply of medieval superstition and to a grossly primitive mentality. Many people, including priests, suggest therefore that exorcisms simply be dropped as "irrelevant" and unbecoming to our enlightened and "modern" religion. As for the non-Orthodox, they go even further: they affirm the need to "demythologize" the New Testament itself, to "liberate" it from an antiquated worldview—of which "demonology" is precisely an essential expression—which only obscures its authentic and eternal message.

It is not our purpose to outline, even superficially, the Orthodox teaching concerning the Devil. In fact, the Church has never formulated it systematically, in the form of a clear and concise "doctrine." What is of paramount importance for us, however, is that the Church has always had the experience of the demonic, has always, in plain words, *known the Devil.* If this direct knowledge has not resulted in a neat and orderly doctrine, it is because of the difficulty, if not impossibility, rationally to define the irrational. And the demonic and, more generally, *evil* are precisely the reality of the irrational. Some theologians and philosophers, in an attempt to explain and thus to "rationalize" the experience and the existence of evil, explained it as an *absence:* the absence of good. They compared it, for example, to darkness, which is nothing but the absence of light and which is dispelled when light appears. This theory was subsequently adopted by deists and humanists of all shades and still constitutes an integral part of our modern worldview. Here the remedy against all evil is always seen in "enlightenment" and "education." For example: explain to teenagers the mechanics of sex, remove the "mystery" and the "taboos," and they will use it rationally, i.e. *well*. Multiply the number of schools and man, who is naturally good, will *ipso facto* live and behave rationally, i.e. *well*.

Such however is certainly not the understanding of evil in the Bible and in the experience of the Church. Here evil is most emphatically *not* a mere *absence*. It is precisely a *presence:* the presence of something dark, irrational and very real, although the origin of that presence may not be clear and immediately understandable. Thus hatred is not a simple absence of love; it is the presence of a dark power which can indeed be extremely active, clever and even creative. And it is certainly not a result of ignorance. We may *know* and hate. The more some men knew Christ, saw His light and His goodness, the more they hated Him. This experience of evil as irrational power, as something which truly takes possession of us and directs our acts, has always been the experience of the Church and the experience also of all those who try, be it only a little, to "better" themselves, to oppose "nature" in themselves, to ascend to a more spiritual life.

Our first affirmation then is that there exists a demonic *reality:* evil as a dark power, as presence and not only absence. But we may go further. For just as there can be no love outside the "lover," i.e. a person that loves, there can be no hatred outside the "hater," i.e. a person that hates. And if the ultimate mystery of "goodness" lies in the person, the ultimate mystery of evil must also be a personal one. Behind the dark and irrational presence of evil there must be a *person* or *persons*. There must exist a personal world of those who have chosen to hate God, to hate light, to be *against*. Who are these persons? When, how, and why have they chosen to be against God? To these questions the Church gives no precise answers. The deeper the reality, the less it is presentable in formulas and propositions. Thus the answer is veiled in symbols and images, which tell of an initial rebellion against God within the spiritual world created by God, among angels led into that rebellion by *pride*. The origin of evil is viewed here not as ignorance and imperfection but, on the contrary, as knowledge and a degree of

perfection which makes the temptation of pride possible.
Whoever he is, the "Devil" is among the very first and the
best creatures of God. He is, so to speak, perfect enough,
wise enough, powerful enough, one can almost say *divine*
enough, to know God and not to surrender to Him—to know
Him and yet to opt against Him, to desire freedom from Him.
But since this freedom is impossible in the love and light
which always lead to God and to a free surrender to Him,
it must of necessity be fulfilled in negation, hatred and
rebellion.

These are, of course, poor words, almost totally inadequate
to the horrifying mystery they are trying to express. For we
know nothing about that initial catastrophe in the spiritual
world—about that hatred against God ignited by pride and
that bringing into existence of a strange and evil reality
not willed, not created by God. Or rather, we know about
it only through our own experience of that reality, through
our own experience of evil. This experience indeed is always
an experience of *fall:* of something precious and perfect
deviated from and betraying its own nature, of the utterly
unnatural character of that fall which yet became an integral
and "natural" part of our nature. And when we contemplate
evil in ourselves and outside ourselves in the world, how
incredibly cheap and superficial appear all rational explanations, all "reductions" of evil to neat and rational theories.
If there is one thing we learn from spiritual experience,
it is that evil is not to be "explained" but faced and fought.
This is the way God dealt with evil. He did not explain it.
He sent His Only-Begotten Son to be crucified by all the
powers of evil so as to destroy them by His love, faith and
obedience.

This then is the way we must also follow. On this way
we inescapably meet the Devil at the very moment we make
the decision to follow Christ. In the baptismal rite, which is
an act of liberation and victory, the exorcisms come first
because on our path to the baptismal font we unavoidably
"hit" the dark and powerful figure that obstructs this path.
It must be removed, chased away, if we are to proceed. The
moment that the celebrant's hand has touched the head of a

child of God and marked it with the sign of Christ, the Devil
is there defending that which he has stolen from God and
claims as his possession. We may not see him but the Church
knows he is here. We may experience nothing but a nice and
warm family "affair," but the Church knows that a mortal
fight is about to begin whose ultimate issue is not explanations and theories but eternal life or eternal death. For
whether we want it or not, know it or not, we are all involved
in a spiritual war that has been raging from the very beginning. A decisive victory, to be sure, has been won by God,
but the Devil has not yet surrendered. On the contrary,
according to the Scripture, it is when mortally wounded and
doomed that he stages the last and most powerful battle.
He can do nothing against Christ, but he can do much against
us. Exorcisms therefore are the beginning of the fight that
constitutes the first and essential dimension of Christian
life.

We *speak* to the Devil! It is here that the Christian
understanding of the *word* as, above all, *power* is made
manifest. In the desacralized and secularized worldview of
the "modern man," speech, as everything else, has been
"devaluated," reduced to its rational meaning only. But in
the biblical revelation, word is always power and life. God
created the world with His Word. It is power of creation
and also power of destruction, for it communicates not only
ideas and concepts but first of all spiritual realities, positive
as well as negative. From the point of view of a "secular"
understanding of speech, it is not only useless, it is indeed
ridiculous to "speak to the Devil," for there can hardly be
a "rational dialogue" with the very bearer of the irrational.
But exorcisms are not explanations, not a discourse aimed
at proving anything to someone who from all eternity hates,
lies and destroys. They are, in the words of St. John Chrysostom, "awesome and wonderful invocations,"[8] an act of
"frightening and horrible" power which dissolves and destroys the evil power of the demonic world:

> The Lord lays thee under ban, O Devil!
> He who came into the world and made His abode among men,
> that He might overthrow thy tyranny and deliver man;

who also upon the Tree did triumph over adverse powers,
when the sun was darkened and the earth did quake,
and the graves were opened, and the bodies of the Saints arose;
who also by death has annihilated Death,
and overthrew him who exercised the dominion of Death,
that is thee, O Devil.
I adjure thee by God, who has revealed the Tree of Life,
and has arrayed in ranks the cherubim and the flaming sword,
which turns all ways to guard it;
Be thou under ban!
For I adjure thee by Him who walks upon the surface
    of the sea as if it were dry land,
and lays under His ban the tempests of the winds;
whose glance dries up the deep,
whose interdict makes the mountains to melt away.
The same now, through us, does lay thee under ban.
Fear, begone and depart from this creature,
and return not again;
neither hide thyself in him either by night or by day;
either in the morning or at noonday;
But depart hence to thine own Tartarus
until the great day of Judgment which is ordained.
Fear thou God who sits upon the Cherubim
    and looks upon the deeps;
before whom tremble Angels and Archangels, Powers,
the many-eyed Cherubim and the six-winged Seraphim,
before whom likewise heaven and earth do quake;
the sea and all that therein is.
Begone and depart from this sealed, newly enlisted
    warrior of God;
for I adjure thee by Him who rides upon the
    wings of the wind,
and makes His ministers a flaming fire.
Begone, and depart from this creature
    with all thy powers and thine angels!

Exorcism is indeed a *poem* in the deepest sense of this word, which in Greek means *creation*. It truly manifests and *does* that which it announces; it makes powerful that which it states; it again fills words with the divine energy from which they stem. And exorcism does all this because it is proferred in the name of Christ; it is truly filled with the power of Christ, who has "broken" into the enemy territory, has assumed human life and made human words His own, because He has already destroyed the demonic power from within.

And thus, having exorcised this evil power, the exorcist makes this supplication:

Look upon Thy servant;
Prove him and search him;
And root out of him every operation of the Devil.
Rebuke the unclean spirits and expel them;
And purify the works of Thy hands.
And exerting Thy trenchant might,
Speedily crush Satan under his feet;
And give him victory over the same,
And over his foul spirits;
That having obtained mercy from Thee,
He may be made worthy to partake of Thy heavenly mysteries...
Receive him into Thy heavenly Kingdom.
Open the eyes of his understanding,
That the light of Thy gospel may shine brightly in him...

Liberation from demonic power is the beginning of man's restoration. Its fulfillment, however, is the heavenly kingdom into which man was received in Christ, so that ascension to heaven, communion with God and "deification" have truly become man's ultimate destiny and vocation.

While exorcising the catechumen, the priest, according to the rubrics, *"breathes thrice upon his mouth, brow and breast."* Breathing is the essential biological function that keeps us alive, a function also that makes us totally dependent on the world. And the world is hopelessly *polluted* with sin, evil and death. In the original Christian worldview, there is no room for our modern dichotomy of the "spiritual" and the "material." It only knows man in his totality, in the organic unity and interdependence of the spiritual and the physical in him. The whole world is poisoned and sick, and the act of liberation therefore is not only "spiritual" but also "physical": it is the purification of the very air we breathe, which, in the act of exorcism, becomes pure again and a gift of God; it is life restored as dependence on God, as that life which God gave to man at the beginning.

And the priest continues:
Expel from him every evil and impure spirit
Which hides and makes its lair in his heart...
The spirit of error, the spirit of guile,
The spirit of idolatry and of every concupiscence;
The spirit of deceit and of every uncleanness
Which operates through the prompting of the Devil.
And make him a reason-endowed sheep
In the holy flock of Thy Christ;

An honorable member of the Church;
A consecrated vessel, a child of the light;
And an heir of Thy Kingdom;
That having lived in accordance with Thy commandments
And preserved inviolate the seal,
And kept his garment undefiled,
He may receive the blessedness of the Saints
In Thy Kingdom. . .

The exorcisms are completed. The first liberation has taken place. Man is restored as a free being capable of true freedom—not that which we call freedom and which in fact makes man a permanent slave of his own desires and appetites, but the freedom to receive again the true life which comes from God and leads to God, the freedom to make the only truly free and truly liberating choice—that of God. It is this choice that constitutes the next step of the baptismal liturgy.

4. The Renunciation of Satan

This rite as well as the one that immediately follows it, the *profession of Christ,* usually took place shortly before Baptism itself, either on Good Friday or Holy Saturday.[9] Thus they constituted the very end and completion of the entire catechetical preparation. In today's rite they are performed immediately after the exorcisms.

Then the priest turns the person who is come to Baptism to face the West, unclad, unshod, and having hands uplifted.

"*. . . to face the West . . .*" The West here is the symbol of darkness, the "side" of Satan.[10] The catechumen truly faces him, for the exorcisms have made him free to renounce, to challenge and to reject him. This very turning to the West is thus an act of freedom, the first free act of the man liberated from enslavement to Satan.

"*. . . unclad, unshod, and having his hands uplifted . . .*" The catechumen is deprived of all that concealed from him his status as a slave, that made him appear to be a free man, not even knowing his enslavement, his misery and

his prison. Now, however, he *knows* that he was a captive—
"and the captives go naked and unshod.""[11] He has put aside
all that masked his captivity, his belonging to Satan. He
"knows from what evil he is being delivered and to what
good he is hurrying . . ."[12] His uplifted hands indicate that
he surrenders to Christ, wants now to be His captive, seeks
the captivity which, according to St. John Chrysostom,
"changes slavery into freedom . . . drives one from foreign
soil and leads him to his homeland, the heavenly Jerusalem. . . ."[13]

> *And the priests says:*
> Dost thou renounce Satan, and all his Angels, and all his works,
> and all his service, and all his pride?
> *And the catechumen makes answer, or his sponsor for him, and says:*
> I do.
> *And this question and answer are thrice repeated.*
> *Again the priest questions the catechumen:*
> Hast thou renounced Satan?
> *And the catechumen, or his sponsor for him, makes answer:*
> I have.
> *And this question and answer likewise are thrice repeated.*
> *Then the priest says:*
> Breathe and spit upon him.

When this rite of renunciation came into existence, its
meaning was self-evident to the catechumen as well as to the
entire Christian community. They lived within a pagan world
whose life was permeated with the *pompa diaboli,* i.e. the
worship of idols, participation in the cult of the Emperor,
adoration of matter, etc.[14] He not only knew what he was
renouncing; he was also fully aware to what a "narrow way,"
to what a difficult life—truly "non-conformist" and radically
opposed to the "way of life" of the people around him—
this renunciation obliged him.

It is when the world became "Christian" and identified
itself with Christian faith and Christian cult that the meaning of this renunciation began to be progressively lost so
as to be viewed today as an archaic and anachronistic rite,
as a curiosity not to be taken seriously. Christians became so
accustomed to Christianity as an integral part of the world,
and to the Church as simply the religious expression of their
worldly "values," that the very idea of a tension or conflict

between their Christian faith and the world faded from their life. And even today, after the miserable collapse of all these so-called "Christian" worlds, empires, nations, states, so many Christians are still convinced that there is nothing basically wrong with the world and that one can very happily accept its "way of life," all its values and "priorities," while fulfilling at the same time one's "religious duties." Moreover, the Church herself and Christianity itself are viewed mainly as aids for achieving a successful and peaceful worldly life, as spiritual therapy resolving all tensions, all conflicts, giving that "peace of mind" which assures success, stability, happiness. The very idea that a Christian has to *renounce* something and that this "something" is not a few obviously sinful and immoral acts, but above all a certain vision of life, a "set of priorities," a fundamental attitude towards the world; the idea that Christian life is always a "narrow path" and a fight: all this has been virtually given up and is no longer at the heart of our Christian worldview.

The terrible truth is that the overwhelming majority of Christians simply do not see the presence and action of Satan in the world and, therefore, feel no need to renounce "his works and his service." They do not discern the obvious idolatry that permeates the ideas and the values by which men live today and that shapes, determines and enslaves their lives much more than the overt idolatry of ancient paganism. They are blind to the fact that the "demonic" consists primarily in falsification and counterfeit, in deviating even positive values from their true meaning, in presenting black as white and vice versa, in a subtle and vicious lie and confusion. They do not understand that such seemingly positive and even Christian notions as "freedom" and "liberation," "love," "happiness," "success," "achievement," "growth," "self-fulfillment"—notions which truly shape modern man and modern society, their motivations and their ideologies—can in fact be deviated from their real significance and become vehicles of the "demonic."

And the essence of the demonic is always *pride, pompa diaboli.* The truth about "modern man" is that whether a law-abiding conformist or a rebellious non-conformist, he is first of all a being full of pride, shaped by pride, worshiping pride and placing pride at the very top of his values.

To renounce Satan thus is not to reject a mythological being in whose existence one does not even believe. It is to reject an entire "worldview" made up of pride and self-affirmation, of that pride which has truly taken human life from God and made it into darkness, death and hell. And one can be sure that Satan will not forget this renunciation, this rejection, this challenge. "Breathe and spit upon him!" A war is declared! A fight begins whose real issue is either eternal life or eternal damnation. For this is what Christianity is about! This is what our choice ultimately means!

5. Allegiance to Christ

And when he has done this, the priest turns him to the East with his hands lowered.

"*. . . turns him to the East . . .*" If facing the West during the renunciation means facing Satan and his darkness, turning now to the East signifies the conversion of man to the Paradise which was planted in the East, his conversion to Christ, the light of the world. "When you renounce Satan," writes St. Cyril of Jerusalem, "utterly breaking all covenant with him, that ancient pact with hell, there is opened to you the Paradise of God, which He planted towards the east and from which our first father was exiled for his sin. The symbol of this is turning from the West to the East, the place of the light."[15]

"*. . . with his hands lowered . . .*" Rebellion against God is now replaced with surrender, submission and peace. "Turn toward the East, lower your hands, stand in reverence": such are the words addressed by the bishop to the catechumens in the old baptismal rite of the Church of Constantinople.[16]

Now the profession of the allegiance to Christ takes place.

Dost thou unite thyself unto Christ?
And the catechumen, or his sponsor for him, makes answer:
I do.

And this question and answer are thrice repeated.

"... *unite thyself unto Christ* ..." The Greek word here is σύνταξις, which means *adherence, attachment,* and which is the exact opposite of ἀπόστασις, used for the renunciation and whose literal meaning is *giving up, parting company with.* The formula thus implies more than some sort of psychological "unity." It is a profession of a personal attachment to Christ, of an enrollment in the ranks of those who serve Christ, of an oath similar to the one taken by soldiers.[17]

> *Then the priest says to the catechumen:*
> Hast thou united thyself unto Christ?
> *And he replies:*
> I have.
> Dost thou believe in Him?
> I believe in Him as King and as God.

This decision and this oath are taken once and for all; they are not to be reconsidered and re-evaluated "from time to time" for "no man, having put his hand to the plow, and looking back, is fit for the Kingdom of God" (Luke 9:62). Such is the meaning of the second questioning: the passage from the present tense to the perfect.

In Christian language this decision is called *faith*. And faith (in Greek *pistis,* in Latin *fides*) has a meaning much deeper than the one given it by some people today—that of intellectual assent to a set of doctrines and propositions. Above all it means *faithfulness,* unconditional commitment, a total belonging to someone who is to be obeyed and followed no matter what happens.

The catechumen confesses his faith in Christ *as King and as God.* The two titles are not synonymous or repetitious. To believe in Christ as God is not sufficient, for the demons themselves believe in Him (James 2:19). To accept Him as King or Lord means precisely the desire and the decision to follow Him, to make one's whole life a service to Him, to live according to His commandments. This is why the earliest Christian confession of Christ was the confession and proclamation of Him as *Kyrios,* the Lord, a term which in the religious and political language of that time implied the idea of an actual and total power demanding unconditional obedience. Christians were persecuted and put to death because they refused to address the title of "Lord" to the Roman Emperor. "Thou alone art Lord," proclaims one of the most ancient of Christian hymns, the Great Doxology, which we sing every morning without understanding the challenge to all earthly powers and "lords" that it contains. To confess Christ as King means that the Kingdom He revealed and inaugurated is not only a Kingdom of some distant future, of the "beyond" and thus never conflicting with or contradicting all our other earthly "kingdoms" and loyalties. We belong to this Kingdom here and now, and we belong to it and serve it before all other "kingdoms." Our belonging, our loyalty to anything in "this world" —be it State, nation, family, culture or any other "value"— is valid only inasmuch as it does not contradict or mutilate our primary loyalty and "syntaxis" to the Kingdom of Christ. In the light of that Kingdom no other loyalty is absolute, none can claim our unconditional obedience, none is the "lord" of our life. To remember this is especially important now when not only the "world" but even Christians themselves so often absolutize their earthly values—national, ethnic, political, cultural—making them the criterion of their Christian faith, rather than subordinating them to the only absolute oath: the one they took on the day of their Baptism, of their "enrollment" in the ranks of those for whom Christ is the only King and Lord.

6. The Confession of Faith

And he recites the Holy Symbol of the Faith.

This means the *Niceo-Constantinopolitan Creed,* adopted at the First Ecumenical Council of Nicea (325), completed at the Second, in Constantinople (381), and serving since as the Church's universal confession of faith. It is important to stress, however, that *creeds* and *symbols of faith* appeared and were used at first in the context of baptismal preparation, as the summary of the instructions given daily to the "baptizands" during the seven weeks before the paschal

celebration of Baptism.[18] One of the most important parts
of these instructions was the teaching of doctrine and the
mystagogy, the explanation of the liturgical "mysteries."
This *traditio symboli,* the handing over of the Church's faith
and life to the catechumens, began in the very first days
of the paschal Lent and was concluded on Good Friday,
after the renunciation of Satan and the "syntaxis" to Christ,
with the *redditio symboli:*[19] the solemn reading by the catechumen of the symbol of faith as the expression now of his
own faith. What the Church gave him he now gives back
to the Church into which he is about to enter. Now the knowledge *about* Christ is to become knowledge *of* Christ; the
truth preserved by the Church in her Tradition is to become
the faith and life of the new member of the Church. It is for
this reason that even today when the whole congregation
recites or sings the Creed, it begins not with "We believe"
but with "I believe." The Church is a body, an organism,
but an organism made up of persons and of their personal
commitments. The entire faith is given to each, and each
one is responsible for the whole faith. Everything in this
common and unchanging faith is to be appropriated personally, to become the power for transforming one's life.

> *And when he has finished the Holy Symbol of the Faith the priest*
> *inquires of him:*
> Hast thou united thyself unto Christ?
> *And he answers:*
> I have.
> *And this question and answer are thrice repeated.*
> Bow down also before Him.
> *And the catechumen bows himself, saying:*
> I bow down before the Father, and the Son, and the Holy Spirit,
> the Trinity, one in essence and undivided.

The renunciation of Satan was "sealed" with breathing
and spitting on him. Our allegiance to Christ now is sealed
with bowing down before the Holy Trinity. "Bowing down"
is an immemorial and universal symbol of reverence, love
and obedience. We are taught today that the dignity and
freedom of man consists precisely in *not* bowing down before
anyone or anything, in man's constant affirmation of himself
as his sole master. But how miserable, how petty is this

"dignity" and this "freedom"! What a caricature of man is this little fellow—worshipped, complimented and adulated by the whole of our "culture" and who thinks that he fulfills himself in this arrogance and self-sufficiency, self-praise and self-content! And how truly noble, truly human and genuinely free are those who still know what it means to bow before the High and the Holy, the True and the Beautiful; who know what reverence and respect are; who know that bowing down before God is the true condition of freedom and dignity. Indeed Christ is the one truly free man, because He was obedient to His Father to the end and did nothing but the Father's will. To join the Church always has meant to enter into Christ's obedience and to find in it the truly divine freedom of man.

". . . the Trinity one in essence and undivided." The knowledge of Christ is the knowledge of His Father and of the Holy Spirit, of God as Trinity. This is the fulfillment of all knowledge and the very content of life eternal. And again, how important it is to remember this today, when so many people make of "Christ" the symbol and the label of their own "human, all too human" values, aspirations and options; reduce "Jesus" to their passing fads and emotions. Let us firmly confess that there can be no true "revival" of religion without a revival first of Christ's own religion, which is that of the Father, whose Son He is, and the Holy Spirit whom He sends from His Father—without, in other terms, a return to the mystery of all mysteries, the revelation of all revelations, the gift of all gifts, and the joy of all joys: the Triune God, the Holy and Life-Creating Trinity in one essence and undivided.

Now the preparation has come to its end. Now everything is ready for the great act itself: that of death and resurrection in the "likeness" of Christ's Death and Resurrection.

"Blessed is God," proclaims the priest, "Who wills that all men should be saved and should come to the knowledge of the Truth. . ." and in the concluding prayer, he makes this ultimate supplication to God:

Call Thy servant to Thy Holy Illumination;
And grant unto him the great grace of Thy Holy Baptism.

Put off from him the old man and renew him unto life everlasting.
And fill him with the power of Thy Holy Spirit,
In the unity of Thy Christ,
That he may be no more a child of the body,
But a child of Thy Kingdom;
Through the good will and grace of Thine Only-Begotten Son,
With whom Thou art blessed, together with Thy Most Holy,
And Good, and Life-Giving Spirit;
Now and ever, and unto ages of ages. Amen.

CHAPTER II

Baptism

1. The Mystery of Water

In our liturgical books, the Office of Holy Baptism is introduced by the following rubric:

The Priest enters the Sanctuary and puts on white garments, and his gauntlets. And when he has lighted all the tapers, he takes the censer and goes to the font, and censes around it; and having given the censer to be held, he makes a reverence.

How many people today realize that this rubric is all that remains from the greatest of all solemnities of the early Church, the paschal celebration of Baptism and the baptismal celebration of Pascha?[1] We stress this again because, even though it is probably impossible simply to reintegrate Baptism into Pascha, the paschal character of Baptism—the connection between Baptism and Pascha—remains the key not only to Baptism but to the totality of the Christian faith itself. The initial rubric reminds us that this paschal character of the celebration must be preserved. This means, first of all, the celebration of Baptism by the Church, i.e. with the participation of the people of God, as an event in which the whole

Church acknowledges herself as *passage—Pascha—*from "this world" into the Kingdom of God, as participation in the decisive events of Christ's Death and Resurrection. The proper celebration of Baptism is indeed the source and the starting point of all liturgical renewal and revival. It is here that the Church reveals her own nature to herself, constantly renews herself as a community of the baptized. And in the light of this essential function of Baptism—always to *renew* the Church—how inadequate and liturgically wrong our short, "private" Baptisms appear, deprived of all solemnity, performed in the absence of the Church, reduced to a bare "minimum." Let us remember then that whenever and wherever Baptism is celebrated, we find ourselves—spiritually at least!—on the eve of Pascha, at the very end of the great and holy "sabbath," at the very beginning of that unique night which every year truly makes us enter into the Kingdom of God.

Baptism begins with a solemn *blessing of water.* But so deep is our liturgical decadence that some priests simply omit this blessing. Why indeed go through this relatively lengthy rite when it is so easy to pour a few drops of the previously blessed "holy water" into the baptismal font and thus satisfy people who are always begging for "shorter services"? In some churches there is even no baptismal font; one performs Baptism by sprinkling the child with a few drops of the "holy water" considered as "necessary and sufficient." Ten minutes, and one is a Christian—a member of the Body of Christ, a consecrated vessel of the Holy Spirit, a fellow citizen with the Saints! All that remains to be done is to issue a baptismal certificate. No wonder then that to more and more people today, not only Baptism, but the whole Church with her incomprehensible and archaic rites seems utterly "irrelevant," and they simply "drop out" and seek elsewhere that spiritual food without which man cannot live.

We must understand, therefore, that it is precisely *water* which reveals to us the meaning of Baptism and that this revelation takes place in the consecration of water before Baptism. Not only does Baptism *begin* with the blessing of water, but it is this blessing alone that reveals all the dimensions of the baptismal mystery, its truly cosmical content and depth. It is, in other terms, the blessing of water that manifests the *relevance* of Baptism, by revealing its relation to the world and matter, to life and all its aspects. And if today, even in theological manuals, Baptism is presented as an almost magical act, if it has ceased to be the source, the constant "term of reference" in both liturgy and piety, it is precisely because it in fact has been disconnected from the "mystery of water," which gives it its real context and significance. It is with this mystery of water, then, that we must begin our explanation.

Water is undoubtedly one of the most ancient and universal of all religious symbols.[2] From the Christian point of view three essential dimensions of this symbolism are important. The first one can be termed *cosmical*. There can be no life without water, and because of this the "primitive" man identifies water with the principle of life, sees in it the *prima essentia* of the world: ". . . and the Spirit of God was moving on the face of the waters" (Gen. 1:2). But if water reflects and symbolizes the world as cosmos and life, it is also the symbol of destruction and death. It is the mysterious depth which kills and annihilates, the dark habitation of the demonic powers, the very image of the irrational, uncontrollable, elemental in the world. The principle of life, a life-giving power, and the principle of death, the power of destruction: such is the essentially ambiguous intuition of water in man's religious worldview. And finally, water is the principle of purification, of cleanliness, and therefore of regeneration and renewal. It washes away stains, it re-creates the pristine purity of the earth. It is this fundamental religious symbolism of water—symbolism rooted in the self-evident and natural attributes of water—that permeates the Bible and the whole biblical story of creation, fall and salvation. We find water at the very beginning, in the first chapter of Genesis, where it stands for creation itself, for the "cosmos" in which the Creator rejoices for it reflects and sings His glory. We find water as wrath, judgment and death in the stories of the Flood and of the annihilation of Pharaoh and his chariots under the waves of the Red Sea. And we find it finally as the means of purification, repentance and forgiveness in the Baptism of St. John, the descent of Christ into the waters of Jordan, and in His ultimate commandment: "go ye and baptize..."[3]

Creation, Fall and Redemption, Life and Death, Resurrection and Life Eternal: all the essential dimensions, the entire content of the Christian faith, are thus united and "held together" in their inner interdependence and unity in this one symbol; and it is indeed the initial and essential meaning, but also the power of this symbol that it "holds together," brings together (σύμβολον, from the Greek συμβάλλω, to bring together) that which was broken, dislocated and mutilated.[4] But thus understood, the blessing of water prior to Baptism ceases to be what it has become so often: a kind of preliminary and optional ceremony aimed at producing the "matter of the sacrament." It is again that which it was from the very beginning: the *epiphany,* the revelation of the true meaning of Baptism as a cosmical, ecclesiological and eschatological act: cosmical, because it is the sacrament of the New Creation; ecclesiological, because it is the sacrament of the Church; eschatological, because it is the sacrament of the Kingdom. It is by entering into this *mystery of water* that we begin to understand why, in order to *save* a man, we must first of all immerse him in water.

2. The Blessing of Water[5]

The blessing of water begins with the solemn doxology: "Blessed is the Kingdom of the Father, and of the Son, and of the Holy Spirit, now and ever, and unto ages of ages. Amen." Today, of all liturgical services only three, Baptism, Marriage and Eucharist, have this doxology as their beginning. All other services begin with "Blessed is our God." This is more than a minor rubric. It reminds us that in the past the sacraments of Baptism and Matrimony not only were celebrated in the context of the eucharistic gathering of the Church, but that the Eucharist was their self-evident "end" and fulfillment. Of this organic connection we shall speak later. But already now we must stress that this doxology announces the Kingdom of God as the theme, the content and the ultimate goal or end of Baptism. We must stress this because for too long a time the link between the very notion of "sacrament" and the central theme, the essential content of the Christian faith—the Kingdom of God—was obscured. The manuals of theology defined the sacraments as "means of grace" but somehow forgot to disclose that "grace" is ultimately nothing else but the gift to us of the Kingdom announced, inaugurated and given by Christ, the possibility to know it and to live by it. They forgot to say, therefore, that each sacrament is, by its very nature and function, a real *passage* into that Kingdom; that the grace it bestows on us is indeed the power which transforms our life by making it both a participation in and a pilgrimage toward the Kingdom of God; that the miracle of grace is always to make our heart love, desire and hope for the new treasure implanted in it. Thus the sacrament is a passage, a journey; and the initial doxology reveals and announces its final destination: the Kingdom of God.

To the Great Litany which follows the opening doxology, special petitions are added:

> That this water may be sanctified with the power and effectual operation and the descent of the Holy Spirit...

In the beginning, the Holy Spirit "moved on the face of the waters," creating the world, transforming chaos into cosmos. It is His descent, His power, His operation that now re-create the fallen world, make it again into cosmos and life.

> That there may be sent down into it the grace of redemption, the blessing of Jordan...

Purified and restored to its original nature, water now is to be more: Christ by His descent into Jordan, by His Baptism, has made it into the power of redemption for all men, the bearer in the world of the grace of redemption.

That there may come upon this water the purifying operation
of the Super-Substantial Trinity. . .

The Baptism of Christ in Jordan was the first epiphany
of the Trinity in the cosmos, the manifestation of the Father,
the Son and the Holy Spirit. To be redeemed, therefore, is
to receive this revelation, to *know* the Trinity, to be in communion with the Triune God.

That we may be illumined by the light of understanding and piety,
and by the descent of the Holy Spirit. . .

Note the plural personal pronoun *we* in this petition.
Baptism is not an affair between the priest and the baptizand.
Just as "this water" represents and stands for the entire
cosmos, the entire Church receives the illumination of the
Holy Spirit, is involved in this act of recreation and redemp-
tion.

That this water may prove effectual unto the averting of every
snare of enemies both visible and invisible. . .

It is through his enslavement to the world and its matter
that man became the slave of the demonic powers. The
liberation of man begins with the liberation, i.e. the purification and the redemption of matter, its restoration to its
original function: to be a means of God's presence and,
therefore, to be a protection and defense against the destruc-
tive "demonic" reality.

That he who is baptized therein may be made worthy of the Kingdom
incorruptible. . .

Baptism is not a magical act adding some supernatural
powers to our natural faculties. It is the beginning of life
eternal itself, which unites us here in "this world" with the
"world to come," makes us even now in this life partakers
of God's Kingdom.

For him who is now come unto Holy Baptism and for his
salvation. . .

The world, the Church, and now this one man and his
salvation! Different in this from human ideologies which,

while glorifying and exalting man, in fact subordinate him
to the world, reduce him to collective, impersonal and
abstract "humanity," the Gospel is always aimed at the
person. It is as if the whole world were created for each man
and the salvation of each man were, in the eyes of God,
more precious than the whole world.

> That he may prove himself a child of the light and an heir
> of eternal good things. . .

"A child of the light," "an heir,"—two fundamental
definitions of membership in the Church. Men have become
slaves and thus children of darkness. Christ brings into
existence a new race whose very principle of existence is
that it has seen light, has received it and made it into its
own life: "In Him was life; and the life was the light of
men" (John 1:4). Men who have no "rights" whatsoever
have been made by divine love *heirs,* possessors, owners of
the eternal Kingdom, given "rights" to it.

> That he may be a member and partaker of the Death and
> Resurrection of Christ our God. . .

Water as death and water as resurrection: not "naturally"
and not "magically" but only inasmuch as the one who is
to be baptized wants—in faith, hope and love—to die with
Christ and to rise with Him from the dead, inasmuch as
Christ's Death and Resurrection have become for him the
decisive event of his own life.

> That he may preserve his baptismal garment and the earnest of
> the Spirit pure and undefiled unto the dread Day of Christ our
> God. . .

That he may remain faithful to his Baptism, living by it,
making it always the source and the power of his life, a
constant judgment, criterion, inspiration, "rule of life."

> That this water may be to him a laver of regeneration unto the
> remission of sins, and a garment of incorruption. . .

That all that the Church knows and reveals to be the
meaning of Baptism be given and received, fulfilled and
appropriated in *this* Baptism, in *this* person.

3. The Priest's Prayer for Himself

Now the priest prays for himself:

O compassionate and merciful God, Who triest the heart and the reins, and Who alone knowest the secret thoughts of men... Thou Who knowest all things concerning me, regard me not with loathing, neither turn Thou Thy face from me; but consider not mine iniquities at this present hour, O Thou Who disregardest man's sins unto his repentance. And wash away the vileness of my body, and the pollution of my soul. And sanctify me wholly by Thine all-perfect, invisible might, and by Thy spiritual right hand; lest, while I proclaim liberty unto others, and administer this rite with perfect faith in Thine unutterable love towards mankind, I myself may become the base slave of sin. Yea, O Master, Who alone art good and full of love toward mankind, let not Thy humble servant be led astray; but send Thou down upon me power from on high, and strengthen Thou me in the administration of Thine impending Mystery which is both great and most heavenly; and create the image of Thy Christ in him who now desires to be born again through my unworthy ministry. And build him up upon the foundation of Thine apostles and prophets, that he may not be overthrown; but implant him firmly as a plant of truth, in thy Holy, Catholic, and Apostolic Church, that he be not plucked out. That as he increases in godliness, through him may be glorified Thine all-holy Name....

This prayer is important because it denounces and corrects the tendency to understand sacraments somewhat "magically," a tendency widespread among the Orthodox and whose spiritual danger and consequences in the life of the Church are often overlooked. Since, according to the Church's teaching, the *validity* of sacraments does not, in any way, depend on either the holiness or the deficiencies of those who perform them, one has come little by little to view and to define sacraments exclusively in terms of "validity," as if nothing else "mattered." The whole point, however, is that the Church does not separate validity from fullness and perfection. "Validity" is merely the condition for fulfillment, but it is this latter that truly "matters." The Baptism of a man like Stalin was probably a perfectly "valid" one. Why then was it not *fulfilled* in his life? Why did it not prevent Stalin from sinking into incredible abomination? The question is not a naive one. If millions of people, "validly" baptized, have left the Church and still leave it, if Baptism seems to have no impact on them whatsoever, is it not, first of all, *because of us,* because of our weakness, deficiencies, minimalism and nominalism, because of our own constant betrayal of Baptism? Is it not because of the incredibly low level of the Church's life, reduced to a few "obligations" and thus having ceased to reflect and to communicate the power of renewal and holiness? All this of course applies above all to the clergy, to the priest, the celebrant of the Church's mysteries. If he himself is not the image of Christ, "by word, by deed, by teaching" (I Tim. 4:12), where is man to see Christ and how is he to follow Him? Thus to reduce sacraments to the principle of "validity" only is to make a caricature of Christ's teaching. For Christ came into this world not that we may perform "valid" sacraments; He gave us valid sacraments so that we may fulfill ourselves as children of light and witnesses of His Kingdom.

The prayer of the priest "for himself" reminds us of this awful responsibility, of our total dependence on one another for spiritual growth and fulfillment. It reveals Baptism to be not an "end in itself" but the beginning of a process in which the whole community, but especially the pastor, is to have a decisive part. It is the process of "creating the image of Christ" in the newly baptized, of "building him up upon the foundation of the apostles and prophets," i.e. of the Christian teaching, of helping him "not to be overthrown" but "to increase in godliness."

In the past, we know it already, not only the candidate alone but the whole Church prepared herself for Baptism. For she knew that by accepting into herself a new member, she accepted the responsibility for his eternal salvation. It is about this responsibility that we hear just at the beginning of the sacramental action.

4. "And show this Water..."

Now we are ready. And the priest, standing before the water as if facing the whole cosmos on the day of creation— as the first man opening his eyes to God's glory and contemplating all that God has done in Christ for our redemption and salvation—proclaims:

> Great art Thou, O Lord, and marvellous are Thy works, and there is no word which suffices to hymn Thy wonders!

This prayer of blessing and consecration of water can be termed a *eucharistic prayer.*[6] It is a solemn act of praise and thanksgiving, an act of adoration by which man, on behalf of the whole world, responds to God. And it is this eucharist and adoration that take us back to the *beginning,* make us indeed witnesses of creation. For thanksgiving is truly the first and the essential act of man, the act by which he fulfills himself as man. The one who gives thanks is no longer a slave; there is no fear, no anxiety, no envy in adoration. Rendering thanks to God, one becomes free again, free in relation to God, free in relation to the world.

> For Thou, of Thine own good will, hast brought into being all things which before were not, and by Thy might Thou upholdest creation, and by Thy providence Thou orderest the world. When Thou hadst joined together the universe out of four elements, Thou didst crown the circle of the year with four seasons. Before Thee tremble all the Powers endowed with intelligence. The sun singeth unto Thee. The moon glorifieth Thee. The stars meet together before Thy presence. The light obeyeth Thee. The deeps tremble before Thee. The water-springs are subject unto Thee. Thou hast spread out the heavens as it were a curtain. Thou hast established the earth upon the waters. Thou hast set round about the sea barriers of sand. Thou hast shed abroad the air for breathing. The Angelic Powers serve Thee. The Choirs of the Archangels fall down in adoration before Thee. The many-eyed Cherubim and the six-winged Seraphim, as they stand round about and fly, veil their faces in awe before Thine ineffable glory...

This is the *Preface* similar to the one which always inaugurates the eucharistic prayer over the Bread and Wine. Preface, *praefatio,* literally means foundation, beginning, that on which everything else depends, that which "makes possible" all that follows. And it is indeed this thanksgiving that takes us back to Paradise, for it restores in us the very principle and essence of our being, life, and knowledge.

And the priest continues:

> For Thou, Who art God inexpressible, existing uncreated before

the ages, and ineffable, didst descend upon earth, and didst take on the semblance of a servant, and wast made in the likeness of man: for, because of the tender compassion of Thy mercy, O Master, Thou couldest not endure to behold mankind oppressed by the Devil; but Thou didst come, and didst save us. We confess Thy grace. We proclaim Thy mercy. We conceal not Thy gracious acts. Thou hast delivered the generation of our mortal nature. By Thy birth Thou didst sanctify a Virgin's womb. All creation magnifieth Thee, who hast manifested Thyself. For Thou, O our God, hast revealed Thyself upon earth, and hast dwelt among men. Thou didst hallow the streams of Jordan, sending down upon them from heaven Thy Holy Spirit and didst crush the heads of the dragons who lurked there. . . .

From the *Preface* we move to the *Anamnesis,* the remembrance, the recapitulation of the saving events by which God has restored human nature, saved the world and manifested His Kingdom. Man has rejected life as given to him by God and by his sin has taken the whole of creation into "oppression by the Devil," into destruction and death. Darkness has replaced light. But God did not forget man. In Christ He Himself has come to save, to restore and to re-create. It is this event of all events—the Incarnation of God— that constitutes forever the *remembrance* of man; and it is this remembrance, i.e. knowledge and acceptance of Christ, faith in Him, communion with Him, that *is* salvation. We are saved by confessing His grace, by proclaiming His mercy, by concealing not His gracious acts, by making, in other terms, our whole life a response to Christ. In man's response, all creation once more becomes the glorification of God, the means of His manifestation, His *epiphany*. The waters of creation, darkened and polluted by the fall, which had become the very symbol of death and demonic oppression, now are revealed as the waters of Jordan, as the beginning of re-creation and salvation. The Holy Spirit, the Giver of Life, who "moved on the face of the waters" in the beginning, descends again on them; and they—and through them the world—are revealed to be that which they were meant and created to be: the life of man as communion with God. The time of salvation begins again, and we are witnesses and partakers of that beginning and we thank God for it.

It is the very essence and function of the Church to manifest and to fulfill this *beginning* always and everywhere, to re-create—in Christ and the Holy Spirit—man by re-creating—in Christ and the Holy Spirit—the world for him:

> Wherefore, O King Who lovest mankind, come Thou *now* and
> sanctify *this* water by the indwelling of Thy Holy Spirit.
> And grant unto it the grace of redemption, the blessing of Jordan.
> Make it the fountain of incorruption, the gift of sanctification,
> the remission of sins, the remedy of infirmities, the final destruction
> of demons, unassailable by hostile powers, filled with angelic
> might. Let those who would ensnare Thy creature flee far from it.
> For we have called upon Thy Name, O Lord, and it is wonderful,
> and glorious, and terrible unto adversaries.

After the *Anamnesis,* the *Epiclesis,* the invocation of the Holy Spirit, Who alone fills with power and reality that which we ask and hope for, Who fulfills our faith, realizes our symbols, gives "grace upon grace," makes water all that He Himself reveals it to be.[7]

> *Then the priest signs the water thrice with the sign of the cross,*
> *dipping his fingers therein, and breathing upon it, he says thrice:*
> Let all adverse powers be crushed beneath the sign of the image
> of Thy cross!

We know already that salvation and restoration begin with an act of *liberation,* i.e. exorcism. First the neophyte was exorcised. Now we exorcise the water, the symbol of both his dependence on the world and his enslavement to the demonic powers:[8]

> We pray Thee, O God, that every aerial and obscure phantom
> may withdraw itself from us; and that no demon of darkness
> may conceal himself in this water; and that no evil spirit which
> instilleth darkening of intentions and rebelliousness of thought
> may descend into it with him who is about to be baptized.

No, these words are not the remnants of some archaic and irrelevant mythology. In the Christian worldview, *matter is never neutral.* If it is not "referred to God," i.e. viewed and used as means of communion with Him, of life in Him, it becomes the very bearer and *locus* of the demonic. It is not an accident that the rejection of God and religion in our time has crystalized as *materialism,* that materialism is proclaimed to be the ultimate scientific "truth," and that in the name of "materialism" an unprecedented war against

God is staged and rages in ever-expanding parts of our supposedly civilized world. But it is also not an accident that pseudo-religion and pseudo-spirituality so often consist in a rejection of matter, and thus of the world itself—so often identify matter with evil, and thus are a blasphemy against God's creation. Only the Bible and the Christian faith reveal and experience matter on the one hand as essentially *good,* yet on the other hand as the very vehicle of man's fall and enslavement to death and sin, as the means by which Satan has stolen the world from God. Only in Christ and by His power can matter be *liberated* and become again the symbol of God's glory and presence, the sacrament of His action and communion with man.

And finally, the *Consecration:*

> But do Thou, O Master of all, *show this water* to be the water of redemption, the water of sanctification, the purification of flesh and spirit, the loosing of bonds, the remission of sins, the illumination of the soul, the laver of regeneration, the renewal of the Spirit, the gift of adoption to sonship, the garment of incorruption, the fountain of life. For Thou hast said, O Lord: Wash ye, be ye clean; put away evil things from your souls. Thou hast bestowed upon us from on high a new birth through water and the Spirit...

"...show this water..." Consecration, be it of water, or of the bread and wine in the Divine Liturgy (cf. in the eucharistic prayer of St. Basil: "and show this bread as the very precious Body..."), is never a visible and "physical" miracle, a change that can be tested and proved by our senses. One can even say that in "this world," i.e. by its standards and "objective" laws, nothing "happens" to water, bread or wine, and no laboratory test could detect any change or mutation in them, so that even to expect such a change, to look for it, has always been considered as blasphemy and sin by the Church. Christ came not to *replace* "natural" matter with some "supernatural" and sacred matter, but to *restore* it and to fulfill it as the means of communion with God. The holy water in Baptism, the bread and wine in the Eucharist, stand for, i.e. *represent* the whole of creation, but creation as it will be at the *end,* when it will be consummated in God, when He will fill all things with Himself.

It is this *end* that is revealed, anticipated, made already *real* to us in the sacrament; and in this sense each sacrament makes us *pass over* into the Kingdom of God. It is because the Church herself is the sacrament of this *passage* and in each of her sacraments takes us *there,* into the Kingdom of God, that the water of Baptism is *holy,* i.e. the very presence of Christ and the Holy Spirit; that the bread and wine of the Eucharist are *truly,* i.e. really, and with a reality more real than all the "objective" realities of "this world," the Body and Blood of Christ, His *parousia,* His presence among us. Thus *consecration* is always the manifestation, the epiphany of that End, of that ultimate Reality for which the world was created, which was fulfilled by Christ through His Incarnation, Death, Resurrection and Ascension, which the Holy Spirit reveals today in the Church and which will be consummated in the Kingdom "to come."

But precisely because consecration is always the manifestation of the end of all things, it is never an "end in itself." The bread and wine are revealed to man as "truly the Body, truly the Blood of Christ" so that he can achieve true communion with God. In the Orthodox Church there is no "adoration" of the Holy Gifts in themselves and for themselves; the fulfillment of the Eucharist is in the communion and transformation of man for which it is given. The water is consecrated so as to *show* and to *be* remission of sins, redemption, salvation; to be that which all matter is meant to be: a means to an end, which is man's deification—knowledge of God and communion with God.

> Wherefore, O Lord, manifest Thyself in this water, and grant that he who is baptized therein *may be transformed;* that he may put away from him the old man, which is corrupt through the lusts of the flesh, and that he may be clothed with the new man, and renewed after the image of Him who created him: that being buried after the pattern of Thy death, in Baptism, he may, in like manner, be a partaker of Thy Resurrection; and having preserved the gift of the Holy Spirit, and increased the measure of grace committed unto him, he may receive the prize of his high calling, and be numbered with the first-born whose names are written in heaven, in Thee, our God and Lord Jesus Christ. For unto Thee are due glory, dominion, honor, and worship, together with Thy Father who is from everlasting, and Thine All-Holy and Good and Life-Giving Spirit, now and ever, and unto ages of ages. Amen.

Such is the meaning of the baptismal blessing of water. It is the re-creation of matter, and thus of the world, in Christ. It is the gift of that world to man. It is the gift of the world as communion with God, as life, salvation, and deification.

5. The Oil of Gladness

Peace be with you all, *says the priest, and* Bow your heads unto the Lord. *And he breathes thrice upon the vessel containing the oil, and makes thrice over it the sign of the cross, as it is held by the deacon.*

After the water is blessed, it is anointed with oil. Like water, oil has always been an essential religious symbol,[9] its symbolic value, as in the case of water, being rooted in its practical significance and use. In the ancient world, oil was used primarily as *medicine.* The Good Samaritan in the Gospel pours oil and wine on the wounds of the man whom he found lying by the road. Oil was also a natural source of *light* and thus of *joy.* Even today the most solemn and joyful part of a festal liturgical vigil is called *polyeleion,* this term referring to both the Greek word ἔλεος, mercy, which is repeated many times in Psalm 135 (136), and to the illumination of the church with "plenty of oil" (ἔλαιον). And finally, oil—symbolizing healing, light and joy—was a symbol of reconciliation and peace: it was an olive branch which a dove brought to Noah to announce God's forgiveness and reconciliation with man after the Flood. This "natural" symbolism of oil determined from the beginning its use in the liturgical life of the Church.

In the pre-baptismal anointment of the water and of the body of the catechumen, oil is above all the symbol of life, but of life not as mere existence, but as fullness, joy and participation in that mysterious and ineffable essence of life which we feel from time to time in moments of happiness and exultation; life of which the Bible speaks when it calls life a gift of the Holy Spirit, the Giver of Life; life as the "light of man"; life as not a synonym but as the *content* of existence; in short, life as participation in divine life itself.

Again, the same order is followed. First, the *exorcism* of oil, its "liberation," its restoration to its true function, as revealed in its "symbolism": such is the meaning of the breathing upon it and its triple blessing with the sign of the cross. Then, an *anamnesis*—the recapitulation of the meaning of oil in the history of salvation—and a *thanksgiving*. We thank God over the oil, and thus we make it again what God has made it: a gift of healing, a gift of peace, a gift of spiritual power and life.

> O Lord and Master, the God of our fathers, Who didst send unto them that were in the ark of Noah Thy dove, bearing in its beak a twig of olive, the token of reconciliation and of salvation from the flood, the foreshadowing of the mystery of grace; and didst provide the fruit of the olive for the fulfilling of thy Holy Mysteries; who thereby fillest them that were under the Law with Thy Holy Spirit, and perfectest them that are under grace: Bless also this holy oil with the power and operation and indwelling of the Holy Spirit, that it may be an anointing unto incorruption, an armor of righteousness, to the renewing of soul and body, to the averting of every assault of the devil, the deliverance from all evil of those who shall be anointed therewith in faith, or who are partakers thereof; unto Thy glory and the glory of Thine Only-Begotten Son, and Thine All-Holy and Good, and Life-Giving Spirit, now, and ever, and unto ages of ages. Amen.

Finally, the *anointment* itself:

> *And the priest, singing* Alleluia *with the people, makes three signs of the cross in the water with the oil.*

Once more creation is achieved, made full and perfect. And there comes the moment when all of it "explodes" in joy and thanksgiving, bears witness to God's glory, reflects His presence and power. This fullness cannot be analyzed or defined; it can only be "thanked for" and proclaimed in this shout of joy which is *Alleluia!* The new creation is here, present in this baptismal font, ready for man as a gift to him of new life, light and power. "Blessed is God," says the priest "who illumines and sanctifies every man that *comes into the world,* now and ever, and unto ages of ages." And to this wonderful testimony the people answer with a solemn confirmation: *Amen!*

Then the person who is to be baptized is presented. The priest takes some of the oil with two fingers, and makes the sign of the cross upon his brow, his breast, and between his shoulders, saying:
The servant of God is anointed with the oil of gladness in the Name of the Father, and of the Son, and of the Holy Spirit. Amen.
And he anoints his breast and shoulders. On the breast saying:
Unto the healing of soul and body.
On the ears:
Unto the hearing of faith.
On the hands:
Thy hands have made me and fashioned me.
On the feet:
That he may walk in the way of Thy commandments.

This is the *re-creation of man:* of his body, his members, his senses. Through sin man has obscured in himself the image and ineffable glory of God. He has lost his spiritual beauty; he has broken the icon. He is to be reshaped and restored. It is not with the "soul" alone that Baptism is concerned; it is with the entire man. Baptism is above all the restoration of man precisely as *wholeness,* the reconciliation of the soul and the body. "The oil of gladness": the same oil on the water and on the body of man for reconciliation with God and, in God, with the world. The same Spirit: the same life, the destruction of all false dichotomies and pseudo-spiritualities, the return to the eternal mystery of creation, ". . .and God saw that it was very good. . ." (Gen. 1:31).[10]

6. "Form" and "Essence"

Having reached the climax of the baptismal liturgy, immersion or Baptism itself, we must pause and try to answer a question on which the whole understanding of this sacrament depends—the understanding, therefore, of its place in the life of the Church as well.

The point of the matter is this: although Baptism has been accepted and practiced always and everywhere as the self-evident beginning and foundation of Christian life, the explanations and interpretations of this fundamental act began at a rather early date to differ from one another. It is as if theologians had difficulties in "holding together" the various aspects of this act, as if human words and categories were not fully adequate to the totality of the baptismal mystery. Thus there appeared a certain discrepancy between Baptism itself—its liturgy, its texts, rites and symbols—on the one hand, and the various theological explanations and definitions of Baptism on the other, between the act and its explanation, the sacrament and its comprehension. This is alarming for if, as we believe, our whole life as Christians depends on Baptism, is given to us in Baptism, and must constantly be referred to Baptism, the proper understanding of this sacrament is not merely an intellectual but indeed an existential necessity for us.

The most striking aspect of this discrepancy is the inability of modern or post-patristic theology to explain the relationship between Baptism and the Death and Resurrection of Christ, a relationship clearly affirmed by both liturgy and Tradition. Not only do they affirm it but they make this relationship the very content and meaning of the sacrament. We are baptized "in the likeness of the Death and Resurrection of Christ... that being buried, after the pattern of Christ's death, in baptism, we may, in the like manner, be partakers of His resurrection" (Rom. 6:5). Hence the emphasis, in the liturgical tradition, on the organic connection between Baptism and Pascha; hence the paschal character of Baptism and the baptismal content of Pascha in the early Church.

This clear affirmation did not remain central, however, when theology began to be understood and developed as a rational explanation and interpretation of the Christian faith. One continued to pay lip service to the baptismal "symbolism" of death and resurrection but the real meaning of the sacrament shifted elsewhere. In virtually every manual of our "systematic" theology the two essential references in explaining Baptism are *original sin* and *grace*. Baptism, we are told, removes from man and liberates him from the original sin, and it also bestows upon him the grace necessary for his Christian life. As all other sacraments, Baptism thus is defined as "means of grace," as a "visible sign of an invisible grace." It is absolutely essential, to be sure, for our salvation; but in these definitions and explanations, it is no longer presented as being truly—in essence and not only in external symbolism—*death* and *resurrection*.[11]

This then is the question we must try to answer: what does Tradition mean when it affirms Baptism to be in the *likeness* and *after the pattern* of Christ's Death and Resurrection, and why in modern theology does this affirmation seem to have lost its focal position? This question in turn implies and presupposes another, broader one: that of the relationship in the sacrament between its *form* and its *essence,* between what is *done*—the liturgical rite—and what the Church believes to *happen,* to be accomplished by means of that "doing." This indeed is the crucial question, for in answering it, the post-patristic theology that still permeates our manuals and catechisms took a path which led it away from the sacramental vision and experience of the early Church and deeply, if not radically, altered the very understanding of sacraments and their place in Christian life.

The simplest way to state the early approach to the sacraments is to say that the Church ignored the dichotomy in them of "form" and "essence," and thus ignored the problem which at a later date became *the* problem of sacramental theology. In the early Church the terms "likeness" and "pattern" most obviously refer to the "form" of Baptism, i.e. to the immersion of the catechumen in water and his rising up from it. Yet it is this very form which manifests, communicates and fulfills the "essence," is its very "epiphany," so that the term "likeness," being the description of the form, is at the same time the revelation of the "essence." Baptism being performed "in the likeness" and "after the pattern" of death and resurrection therefore *is* death and resurrection. And the early Church, before she explains— if she explains them at all—the "why," the "what," and the "how" of this baptismal death and resurrection, simply knew that to follow Christ one must, at first, die and rise again with Him and in Him; that Christian life truly begins with an *event* in which, as in all genuine events, the very distinction between "form" and "essence" is but an irrelevant

abstraction. In Baptism—because it is an event—the form and
the essence, the "doing" and the "happening," the sign and
its meaning coincide, for the purpose of one is precisely to
be the other, both to reveal and to fulfill it. Baptism *is* what
it *represents* because what it represents—death and resurrection—is *true*. It is the representation not of an "idea" but
of the very content and reality of the Christian faith itself:
to believe in Christ is to "be dead and have one's life hid
with Him in God" (Col. 3:3). Such is the central, overwhelming and all-embracing experience of the early Church,
an experience so self-evident, so direct, that at first she did
not even "explain" it but saw it rather as the source and
the condition of all explanations, all theologies.

One can say without any exaggeration that a new chapter
began in the history of the Church when theology broke
the "wholeness" of this initial sacramental vision and experience, and broke it precisely by positing as the preliminary
condition for the proper "understanding" of sacraments the
distinction in them between the "form" and the "essence";
when, in other words, it decided that the "essence" of a sacrament can and even must be known, determined, and defined
apart from its "form." In this short essay we cannot deal
with the historical and spiritual factors which brought about
this decisive change, this—in our eyes at least—"original sin"
of all modern, post-patristic, westernized theology. What is
important for us here is that this change progressively led
to an entirely different understanding of sacraments in
general and of Baptism in particular.

This new approach preserved, to be sure, the crucial
importance of the sacramental "form," yet for reasons quite
different from those of the early Church. In the early Tradition the form is important because its very nature and
function is "epiphanic," because it reveals the essence, truly
is and *fulfills* it. And being the epiphany of the essence,
the form is the means of its knowledge and explanation. In
the new approach, the form is no longer an "epiphany,"
but only the external sign and thus the guarantee that a
particular "essence" has been duly bestowed and communicated. As to this "essence" itself, it can and must be

known and defined apart from the "form" and even prior
to it, for otherwise one would not know what is being
"signified" and "guaranteed" by means of the form. To
use one of the key terms of this new sacramental theology,
the form is that which makes a sacrament *valid* but not the
revelation of *that which is made valid* in the sacrament.

It is very significant indeed that virtually all controversies
concerning the "form" of Baptism—immersion versus sprinkling, baptismal formula, etc.—were centered almost exclusively on the issue of validity and not on that of meaning
or essence.[12] Even those, for example, who defend—and
rightly so—immersion as the proper form of Baptism and
denounce sprinkling as "heresy," do this on purely formal
grounds: sprinkling is a deviation from the practice of the
early Church, considered as an ultimate authority and norm
of validity. Yet the position of those who favor and defend
"sprinkling" stems in fact from the same type of reasoning.
The early Church, they say, while unquestionably practicing
immersion, *also* knew sprinkling—in emergencies, clinical
baptisms, etc.; immersion, therefore, cannot be considered
as *the* condition of validity. The question of essence or meaning is not raised here because both factions, in fact, agree
on it and also agree that it does not depend on the question
of "form." And yet such quarrels about "validity" reveal
better than anything else the profound damage done by this
new approach to the entire sacramental vision and experience
of the Church.

The real tragedy is that by applying the dichotomy of
"form" and "essence" to the sacraments, and by reducing
the notion of "form" to that of "validity," this new sacramental theology ultimately altered and deeply impoverished
the notion of the "essence" itself. There was apparently
nothing new in defining this essence as *grace,* a very scriptural
and traditional term indeed, which the early Church
also frequently used in the explanation of the sacraments.
In reality, however, this term acquired new connotations and
a kind of "self-sufficiency" which it did not have before;
and it acquired them precisely because of its identification
with "essence" as distinct from the "form." In the early

Church *grace* meant above all that very victory over all dichotomies—"form" and "essence," "spirit" and "matter," "sign" and "reality"—which is made manifest in the sacrament and, indeed, in the whole life of the Church and which ultimately *is* the victory of Christ Himself, in whom and by whom the "forms" of this world can truly be, truly communicate, truly fulfill that which they "represent": the epiphany, in "this world" of the Kingdom of God and of its "new life." Thus the grace of Baptism was this very event: a man dying and rising again "in the likeness" and "after the pattern" of Christ's Death and Resurrection; it was the gift to him not of "something" resulting from these events, but of that unique and totally new possibility: truly to die with Christ, truly to rise again with Him so that he may "walk in the newness of life." All this was grace: the "likeness" revealed and experienced as "reality," the baptismal death manifesting again the destruction of death by Christ, the baptismal resurrection "making sure" again Christ's resurrection, becoming the very gift of the new life which shone forth from the grave. All this was grace! And because all this *is* grace, the early Church—while constantly proclaiming it and referring the whole of her life to it—never felt the need to explain grace "in itself" as something that exists, that can be known, defined and even measured apart from these very "epiphanies" whose unique meaning and purpose was to transcend and to heal all "brokenness," all "dichotomies," and thus truly to unite the human to the divine in the "newness of life."

Gradually, however, this understanding of grace began to change. Once the distinction between "form" and "essence" —between the sacrament as "means of grace" and grace itself—came to be accepted as natural and self-evident, the "essence" ceased to be understood as the very fulfillment and the actualization of the "means," the "visibility" of the invisible. It began to be construed, defined and analyzed as an "essence-in-itself," as something given and received through all kinds of "means of grace" yet distinct from each of them.[13] The Christian West, where this whole approach originated and developed, brought it to its logical conclusion: as is well known it ended up by defining grace as a *created* substance, thus distinct from both God and the world, although aimed at guaranteeing orderly communications between them. As to the Orthodox East, while denouncing the doctrine of "created grace" as a Western heresy and thus preserving doctrinal Orthodoxy, it adopted for all practical intents the very same approach in its own, deeply Westernized sacramental theology. Here also an abstract "grace" replaced the concrete "event" as the focus of theological explanations of the sacraments, leaving to their "form" the function, equally abstract after all, of assuring "validity."

One can understand now why this new "systematic theology" virtually abandoned the explanation of Baptism in terms of death and resurrection, so "self-evident" in the early Tradition. For the whole point is that in this new approach there is, so to speak, no interest in either death or resurrection. It is certainly not Christ who dies, for having died and risen again once and for all, Christ "dies no more, death has no dominion over Him" (Rom. 6:9). And it is not man who dies, for even if Baptism is "in the likeness" and "after the pattern" of Christ's Death and Resurrection, its real meaning and validity, according to this approach, is that it bestows "grace." This grace, as the "grace" of all sacraments, may be the *fruit* of Christ's sacrificial Death and Resurrection, the communication to man of their saving power and virtue; but it is not itself an *event* which can and must be termed, not symbolically, not allegorically, but *essentially* death and resurrection.

One can also understand why we call this approach a tragedy and see in it a radical impoverishment of the sacramental vision and experience of the Church. If, for so many people today, sacraments have become incomprehensible "obligations" which they have to fulfill, some once in a lifetime and some once a year; if very few experience them as the joyful source, the very food of their life as Christians; if, in fact, many are those who plainly ask, "why sacraments at all?" or seek to "revalorize" them with all kinds of new meanings and new symbols, is it not above all because theology itself made them into such "obligations," into—let us frankly say—incomprehensible "means" of an equally incomprehensible "grace"? Is it not because, as a result of this, both faith and piety ceased to know and to experience them as true events of that "newness of life" in Christ which *is* grace? While theologians defined and measured the grace and its "operation" in each sacrament, while canonists discussed the forms and conditions of "validity," the faithful—and this is not an exaggeration—"lost interest" in the sacraments. Told that the sacraments are necessary, they accept them as a self-evident ecclesiastical institution; yet not only do they usually not know, but what is much more serious, they also are not really interested in knowing why they are necessary. They would do anything to have their children baptized and thus "made" Christians, but how many among them truly care to understand *how* does Baptism make a Christian, *what* truly happens in Baptism and *why?*

7. "In the Likeness of Christ's Death and Resurrection"

As to the early Church she knew, and she knew it even before she could express and explain this knowledge in rational and consistent theories. She knew that in Baptism we truly die and truly rise again with Christ because she experienced this in her baptismal mystery. To this sacramental knowledge which illumined the whole life of the early Church with ineffable joy, made the whole of it truly paschal and truly baptismal, we must return if we want Baptism to recover its original place and function in the Church. And thus the ultimate questions: *How* do we die in the likeness of Christ's Death? *How* do we rise again in the pattern of His Resurrection? And why is this, and this alone, our entrance into the new life in Him and with Him?

The answer to these questions is contained in the essential truth about Christ's own death as *voluntary* death. "...I lay down my life that I might take it again. No man takes it from me but I lay it down of myself. I have power to lay it down and I have power to take it again" (John 10:17-18).

The Church teaches us that in His sinless humanity Christ was not "naturally" subject to death, was totally free from the human mortality that is our common and inescapable fate. He did not have to die. Therefore, if He died it is only because He wished to die, chose to die, decided to die. And it is the voluntary nature and character of that death, the death of the Immortal One, that makes it a saving death, makes it our salvation, fills it with saving power. But then, before we can answer the question about the relationship between Christ's death and our own baptismal death, we must recover the true significance of Christ's *desire to die.*

I say "recover" because, strange as it may seem, the great "heresy" of our time precisely concerns death. It is here, in this preoccupation so obviously central for both faith and piety, that a paradoxical, although almost unconscious, metamorphosis seems to have taken place, which has virtually removed from our worldview the essentially Christian view and experience of death. To put it in simple, if not somewhat oversimplified terms, this heresy consists in the progressive abandonment by Christians themselves of the *spiritual meaning and content of death*—of death as above all a spiritual and not only "biological" reality. To an overwhelming majority of Christians death means exclusively physical death, the end of *this* life. Beyond that end faith posits and affirms *another,* purely spiritual and endless life— the life of the immortal soul—death being thus a natural passage from the one into the other. In this approach, which in fact is not different from the entire Platonic, idealistic and spiritualistic tradition, what becomes less and less "comprehensible," less and less "existential," what less and less permeates faith, piety and life, is the initial Christian emphasis on the *destruction* of death by Christ ("trampling down death by death"), the uniquely Christian joy, so manifest in the early Church, at the *abolition* of death (". . . Death is swallowed up in victory. O death, where is thy sting? O grave, where is thy victory?" I Cor. 15:54-55), so obvious still in our liturgical tradition ("Christ is risen and not one dead remains in the grave"). It is as if Christ's Death and Resurrection were "events in themselves," to be

commemorated, celebrated, rejoiced about, especially on Good
Friday and Easter, but without any real "existential" connection with our own death and after-death, which we
approach and comprehend within an entirely different per-
spective: that of "natural" or biological death, that of an
equally "natural," although "spiritual," immortality. Death
concerns the body; immortality concerns the soul. And a
Christian, while not overtly rejecting the initial faith and
duly celebrating it, in reality does not know what to make
of the "destruction of death" and "the resurrection of the
body"; he does not know how to relate these notions to his
life experience and his mental universe, which can easily
combine (as it does in the pseudo-spiritual revivals of our
time) positivism and spiritualism, but which is almost totally
closed to the cosmical and eschatological experience of the
early Church.

The reasons for this discrepancy, for this all-pervasive,
although almost unconscious "heresy," are rather obvious.
They are, to use a modern term, "semantic," although on a
very deep psychological and spiritual level. The modern man,
even a Christian, whose understanding of death is entirely
"biological," does not hear the Christian Gospel about the
"destruction" and the "abolition" of death, because on this
"biological" level nothing indeed has happened to death
after Christ's Death. Death has neither been destroyed nor
abolished. It remains the same inescapable and natural law
for saints and sinners, believers and unbelievers alike, the
same organic principle of the world's very existence. The
Christian Gospel does not seem to apply to death as the
modern man understands it, and so he quietly abandons that
Gospel and returns to the old and much more "acceptable"
dichotomy: mortality of the body, immortality of the soul.

What the modern man does not understand, that to which
he has become blind and deaf, is thus the fundamental Christian vision of death, in which the "biological" or physical
death is not the *whole* death, not even its ultimate essence.
For in this Christian vision, death is above all a *spiritual
reality,* of which one can partake while being alive, from
which one can be free while lying in the grave. Death here

is man's *separation from life,* and this means from God Who is the only Giver of life, Who Himself *is* Life. Death is the opposite term, not of immortality—for just as he did not create himself, so also man has no power to annihilate himself, to return to that *nihil* from which he was called into existence by God, and in this sense he is immortal—but of the true life "which was the light of man" (John 1:2). This true life man has the power to reject and thus *to die* so that his very "immortality" becomes eternal death. And this life he has rejected. This is the *Original Sin,* the initial cosmical catastrophy about which we know not "historically," not rationally but by means of that "religious sense," that mysterious inner certitude in man which no sin could ever destroy, which makes him always and everywhere seek salvation.

Thus the *whole* death is not the biological phenomenon of death but the spiritual reality whose "sting... is sin" (I Cor. 15:56)—the rejection by man of the only true life given to him by God. "Sin entered the world and death by sin" (Rom. 5:12): there is no other life but God's life; the one who rejects it *dies* because life without God is *death.* This is the spiritual death, the one that fills the entire life with "dying" and, being separation from God, makes man's life solitude and suffering, fear and illusion, enslavement to sin and enmity, meaninglessness, lust and emptiness. It is this spiritual death that makes man's physical death truly death, the ultimate fruit of his death-filled life, the horror of the biblical "sheol" where the very survival, the very "immortality" is but the "presence of the absence," a total separation, total solitude, total darkness. And as long as we do not recover this Christian vision and "feeling" of death, of death as the horrible and sinful law and content of our life (and not only of our "death"), of death as "reigning" in *this world* (Rom. 5:14), we will not be able to understand the significance of Christ's Death for us and for the world. For it is this spiritual death that Christ came to destroy and to abolish; it is from this spiritual death that He came to save us.

Only now, having said all this, can we comprehend the

crucial meaning of Christ's *voluntary* death, of His *desire*
to die. Man died because he *desired* life for himself and in
himself, because, in other terms, he *loved* himself and his
life more than God, because he preferred something else to
God. His desire is the true content of his sin and therefore
the real root of his spiritual death, its very "sting." But
Christ's life is made up entirely, totally, exclusively of His
desire to save man, to free him from that death into which
man transformed his life, to restore him to that life which
he lost in sin. His desire to save is the very movement,
the very power of that perfect *love* for God and man, of
that total obedience to God's will, the rejection of which
led man to sin and death. And thus His whole life is truly
"deathless." There is no death in it because there is no
"desire" to have anything but God, because His whole life
is in God and in God's love. And because His desire to die
is but the ultimate expression and fulfillment of that love
and obedience—because His death is nothing but love,
nothing but the desire to destroy the solitude, the separation
from life, the darkness and the despair of death, nothing but
love for those who are dead—*there is no "death" in His
death*. His death, being the ultimate manifestation of love
as life and of life as love, removes from death its "sting"
of sin and truly destroys death as the power of Satan and
sin over the world.

He does not "abolish" or "destroy" the physical death
because He does not "abolish" *this world* of which physical
death is not only a "part" but the principle of life and even
growth. But He does infinitely more. By removing the sting
of sin from death, by abolishing death as a spiritual reality,
by filling it with Himself, with His love and life, He makes
death—which was the very reality of separation and corruption of life—into a shining and joyful "passage"—pass-
over—into fuller life, fuller communion, fuller love. "For
to me to live is Christ," says St. Paul, "and to die is gain"
(Phil. 1:21). It is not of the immortality of his soul that
he speaks, but of the new, the totally new meaning and
power of death—of death as "being with Christ," of death
as having become, in this mortal world, the sign and the

power of Christ's victory. For those who believe in Christ
and live in Him, "death is no more," "death is swallowed
up in victory" (I Cor. 15:54) and each grave is filled not
with death, but with life.

We can now return to Baptism and to the question we
raised about its being in the *likeness* of Christ's Death and
Resurrection and about the real meaning of that likeness. For
only now can we realize that the *likeness*—before it is
fulfilled in the rite—*is in us:* in our faith in Christ, in our
love for Him and, therefore, in our desire for that which
He desired. To believe in Christ means, has always meant,
not only to *acknowledge* Him, not only to *receive* from Him
but above all *to give oneself to Him.* Such is the meaning
of His commandment that we should follow Him. And
there is no other way of believing in Him but by accepting
His faith as our faith, His love as our love, His desire as our
desire. For there is no Christ "apart" from that faith, love
and desire; only through them can we know Him Who
is that faith and obedience, love and desire. To believe in
Him and not to believe in what He believed, not to love
what He loved and not to desire what He desired, is *not* to
believe in Him. To separate Him from the "content" of His
life, to expect miracles and help from Him without doing
what He did, and finally to call Him "Lord" and worship
Him without fulfilling the will of His Father, is *not* to
believe in Him. We are saved not because we believe in His
"supernatural" power—such faith He does not want from
us—but because we accept with our whole being and make
ours the *desire* that fills His life, which *is* His life and
ultimately makes Him descend into death to abolish it.

The desire for such a fulfillment and realization of faith
that it can truly be termed and experienced as *death* and
resurrection is thus the very first fruit and "work" of faith
itself, of its *likeness* to Christ's faith. It is indeed impossible
to know Christ without desiring a radical liberation from
"this world," which Christ revealed as being enslaved to sin
and death and to which, while living in it, He Himself was
truly *dead:* dead to its self-sufficiency, to the "lust of the
flesh, and the lust of the eyes, and the pride of life" (I John

2:16) which fill and determine it, and to the "spiritual
death" reigning in it. It is impossible to know Christ without
desiring to be with Him where He is. And He is not in
"this world" whose "fashion is passing away." He is not a
"part" of it. He ascended to *heaven,* not to any "other
world," for heaven—in Christian faith—is not an "outside,"
but the very reality of life in God, of life totally free from
mortal sinfulness and sinful mortality, from that separation
from God which is *the* sin of "this world" and condemns
it to death. To be with Christ is to have that new life—with
God and in God—which is "not of this world"; and this is
impossible unless, in the words of St. Paul—words so simple
yet so incomprehensible to the modern Christian—we "are
dead and our life is hid with Christ in God" (Col. 3:3).
Finally, it is impossible to know Christ without desiring to
drink of the cup that He drinks of, and to be baptized with
the baptism that He is baptized with (Matt. 20:22), without
desiring, in other words, that ultimate encounter and fight
with sin and death which made Him "lay down His life"
for the salvation of the world.

Thus faith itself not only leads us to desire death with
Christ but indeed *is* that very desire. And without it, faith
is no longer faith but a mere "ideology," as questionable,
as contingent as any other "ideology." It is faith that *desires*
Baptism; it is faith that *knows* it to be truly dying and truly
rising with Christ.

8. Baptism

Only God can respond to this desire and fulfill it. Only
He can "grant our heart's desire and fulfill all our mind."
Where there is no faith and no desire there can be no
fulfillment. Yet the fulfillment is always a free gift from
God: *grace* in the deepest meaning of this word. The sacrament then is precisely this: *the decisive encounter of faith
and the Divine response to it, the fulfillment of the one by
the other.* Faith, by being desire, makes the sacrament *possible,* for without faith it would have been "magic"—a

totally extrinsic and arbitrary act destroying man's freedom. But only God, by responding to faith, fulfills this "possibility," makes it truly that which faith desires: dying with Christ, rising again with Him. Only through God's free and sovereign grace do we know, in the words of St. Gregory of Nyssa, "this water truly to be for us both tomb and mother. . ."

Here one objection can be foreseen. How, one may ask, can all this be applied to infant Baptism, to children who obviously have neither personal and conscious faith nor personal "desire"? In fact this is a "helpful" objection, for it is by answering it that we may grasp the ultimate meaning and depth of the Sacrament of Baptism. First of all, the question ought not to be linked to children alone but indeed extended to every Baptism. If what we have just said about faith and desire were understood as implying that the reality and the efficacy of Baptism *depends* on personal faith, is contingent upon the conscious desire of the individual, then the "validity" of each Baptism, be it infant or adult, should be questioned. For to whom is it given to measure faith, to pass judgment on the degree of "comprehension" and "desire" in it?

If the Orthodox Church remained alien to the long Western debate on infant versus adult Baptism, it is because she, in the first place, never accepted the reduction of faith to "personal faith" alone which made that debate inevitable. From the Orthodox point of view, the essential question about faith in its relationship to the sacrament is: *what* faith, and even more precisely, *whose* faith? And the equally essential answer to this question is: *it is Christ's faith,* given to us, becoming our faith and our desire, the faith by which, in the words of St. Paul, "Christ may dwell in your hearts. . . that being rooted and grounded in love (we) may be able to comprehend with all saints what is the breadth and length and depth and height" (Eph. 3:17-18). There is a difference—not only in degree but also in essence—between the faith which *converts* an unbeliever or a non-Christian to Christ, and the faith which constitutes the very life of the Church and of her members and which

St. Paul defines as having in us Christ's mind, i.e. His faith, His love, His desire. Both are gifts of God. But the former is a *response* to God's call while the latter is the very *reality* of that to which the call summons. The Galilean fisherman who, upon being called, leaves his nets and follows Jesus does it on faith; he already believes in the One Who called him, but he does not yet know and possess the faith of the One Who called him. It is his personal faith in Christ which brings the catechumen to the Church; it is the Church that will instruct him in and bestow upon him Christ's faith by which she lives. Our faith in Christ, Christ's faith in us: the one is the fulfillment of the other, is given to us so that we may have the other. But when we speak of the Church's faith—the one by which she lives, which truly *is* her very life—we speak of the presence in her of Christ's faith, of Him Himself as perfect faith, perfect love, perfect desire. And the Church is life because she is Christ's life in us, because she believes that which He believes, loves that which He loves, desires that which He desires. And He is not only the "object" of her faith, but the "subject" of her entire life.

We can now return to the objection mentioned above and which, as we have seen, concerns the Baptism not only of children but of adults as well. For now we know why Baptism does not and indeed cannot "depend" for its *reality* (i.e. for truly being our death, our resurrection with Christ) on personal faith, however "adult" or "mature" it may be. This is not because of any deficiencies or limitations of that personal faith, but only because Baptism depends —totally and exclusively—on Christ's faith; is the very gift of His faith, its true *grace*. "As many of you as have been baptized into Christ have put on Christ," says St. Paul (Gal. 3:27); but what does it mean "to put on Christ" if not that in Baptism we receive His life as our life and thus His faith, His love and His desire as the very "content" of our life? And the presence in this world of Christ's faith is the Church. She has no other life but Christ's, no other faith, no other love, no other desire but His; she has no other task in the world but to communicate Christ to us.

Therefore it is the Church's faith—or, better to say, it is the Church as Christ's faith and life—that makes Baptism both *possible* and *real* as our participation in Christ's death, as our partaking of His resurrection. Thus it is on the faith of the Church that Baptism "depends"; it is the faith of the Church which *knows* and *desires* it to be—and therefore makes Baptism that which it is—both "tomb" and "mother."

All this is evident in the traditional baptismal practice of the Church. On the one hand, she not only admits newly-born children (i.e. those who can have no "personal faith") to Baptism; she indeed requests that they be baptized. Yet, on the other hand, she does not baptize all children but only those who already *belong* to her either through parents or responsible sponsors, who, in other terms, are presented to Baptism from *within* the community of faith. That the Church considers such children as *belonging* to her is proved by the *rite of churching* which, properly understood, applies precisely to non-baptized children of Christian parents. But she would not "steal" children from non-Christian parents; she would not baptize them "behind their parents' backs" without at least the explicit agreement of those who have the real possibility of keeping and bringing them up within the Church. In fact the Church would not consider such Baptisms as "valid." Why? Because if the Church *knows* that all men need Baptism, she also knows that the "newness of life" which Baptism bestows is fulfilled only in the Church, or rather that the Church *is* that life, so radically different from the life of "this world" that it is "hidden with Christ in God" —that, in other terms, although it is bestowed on a person, Baptism has the Church as its reality and fulfillment. Therefore she baptizes only those whose *belonging* to her is explicit and can be ascertained: it is the "personal faith" and its confession in the case of the catechumen; it is, in the case of children, the promise and the confession of those members of the Church—parents or sponsors—who have the power to offer their child to God and to be responsible for his growth in the "newness of life."

Now we are ready for Baptism itself:

When his whole body is thus anointed, the priest baptizes him,
holding him upright, and looking toward the east, as he says:
The servant of God is baptized in the Name of the Father, Amen.
And of the Son, Amen. And of the Holy Spirit, Amen.
At each invocation he immerses him and raises him again.

Such is the *sacrament:* the gift of Christ's Death and
Resurrection to each one of us, the gift which *is* baptismal
grace. It is the gift, the grace of our participation in an
event which, because it took place for us and is our salvation,
was aimed at each one of us, was from the beginning and
totally a gift which can and must be received, accepted,
loved and appropriated by each one of us. In Baptism, the
Death and Resurrection of Christ are truly fulfilled as His
Death *for me,* His Resurrection *for me,* and therefore *my*
death in Christ and *my* resurrection in Him.

The "Amen" with which the entire Church "seals" each
of the three immersions is the testimony that we have seen
and experienced once more that Christ truly died and truly
rose again from the dead so that in Him we may die to
our mortal life and be partakers—here and now—of the
"day without evening." What does it mean indeed to believe
in the resurrection on the last day if one does not taste of
that which makes the resurrection a joyful certitude?

It is because we have seen all this, have been once more
made witnesses of "these things," that we now sing the
joyful *Psalm 32:*

Blessed is he whose unrighteousness is forgiven, and whose sin
is covered. Blessed is the man unto whom the Lord imputeth no
sin, and in whose spirit there is no guile...

This psalm thus is the continuation and the expanding of
the solemn "Amen." Once more we have been made witnesses of divine mercy and forgiveness, of the re-creation
of the world and of man in it. Once more we are at the
beginning—a new man made again into the likeness of
Him who made him, in a new world filled with divine glory:

...Be glad, O ye righteous, and rejoice in the Lord; and be
joyful all ye that are true of heart.[14]

CHAPTER III

The Sacrament
of the Holy Spirit

1. The White Garment

Immediately after the triple immersion the newly baptized is vested in a *white garment,* which in liturgical texts and patristic explanations is also called *shining garment,*[1] *royal robe,*[2] *garment of immortality,*[3] etc.

> *As the priest puts this garment on the catechumen he says:*
> The servant of God is clothed with the robe of righteousness in the Name of the Father, and of the Son, and of the Holy Spirit. Amen.
> *And the following hymn is sung:*
> Vouchsafe unto me the robe of light, O Thou Who clothest Thyself with light as with a garment, Christ, our God, plenteous in mercy.

This is one of the most ancient rites of the baptismal liturgy, and in early explanations of Baptism it occupied quite an important place.[4] In time, however, these explanations, the very understanding of the rite, were "watered down," reduced to a purely external symbolism. The white garment, we are told, symbolizes the spiritual purity and

71

the righteousness for which each Christian must strive in his life. And although there is obviously nothing wrong with this explanation, its deficiency, common in fact to all such symbolic explanations, is that it leaves unanswered the main question: what is the very nature, the very "content" of that purity and righteousness? Yet, and we know it already, it belongs to the essence of the liturgy, of its every rite and action, that they not only "symbolize" something, but are both the *revelation* and the *gift* of that which they symbolize. Thus the rite of the white garment is not merely a reminder of and a call to a pure and righteous life, for if it were only that, it would indeed add nothing to Baptism: it is self-evident that we are baptized in order to lead a Christian life, which, in turn, must be as "pure" and "righteous" as possible. What it reveals and therefore communicates is the radical *newness* of that purity and righteousness, of that *new* spiritual life for which the neophyte was regenerated in the baptismal immersion and which will now be bestowed upon him through the "seal of the gift of the Holy Spirit."

There is no need to prove that today we live in the midst of a deep moral and spiritual crisis. On the one hand, we hear lamentations about the "moral crisis," on the nature of which and the measures to be taken for its solution Christians themselves seem to be deeply divided. Those who defend the "good old" moral code and call for its restoration are opposed by those who denounce its hypocrisy and legalism and advocate a new morality which they call "situation ethics," "ethics of love," etc. On the other hand, there is taking place today a significant revival of interest in, and of a search for, "spirituality"—this word covering an incredible and precisely spiritual confusion which, in turn, generates a great variety of dubious spiritual "teachings" and "recipes." We have a world-affirming spirituality ("celebration of life") and a world-denying spirituality ("the end of the world"), the ecstatic "Jesus movement" and the ecstatic "charismatic movement," the multiplication of "elders" and "gurus" of all kinds, "transcendental meditation," the "gift of tongues," "Oriental mysticism," rediscovery of the Devil and "witchcraft," obsession with "exorcisms," etc. And, on the level of our parishes not yet touched by these fashionable and "avant-garde" spiritual trends, we still have the age-old reduction of Christian life to various external "obligations" and "taboos"—the compliance with which does not in the least prevent our "good people" from living in fact a perfectly secularized life and from abiding by criteria and norms almost totally alien to the Gospel.

All this, I repeat, reveals such an abysmal confusion, such a lack of genuine spiritual criteria and, above all, *sobriety*—which in the Orthodox tradition is always posited as the *conditio sine qua non* of all genuine spirituality—that even the most authentic search is in danger of being misdirected and led into a spiritual catastrophe. Our time is the time of imposture, of spiritual fraud and counterfeit taking the form of an "angel of light" (II Cor. 11:14). And the main danger, the main deficiency of this whole phenomenon is that too many people today—including the seemingly most traditional "dispatchers" of spirituality—seem to view "spirituality" as a kind of entity in itself, almost totally disconnected from the entire Christian view and experience of God, world and man, from the totality of Christian faith. I have seen the *Philocalia* read and practiced in groups and circles whose esoteric teachings not only have nothing in common with but are diametrically opposed to the Christian worldview. Thus, when disconnected from the totality of faith, even that "spirituality" which has the most traditional, the most Orthodox appearance is always in danger of becoming one-sided, reductionist and in this sense *heretical* (from the Greek αἵρεσις: choice and, therefore, reduction) —of becoming, in other terms, pseudo-spirituality.

The danger of such pseudo spirituality has always existed. It is already denounced by St. John, who begs Christians not "to believe every spirit, but try the spirits whether they are from God" and establishes the fundamental rule for such "trying": "Every spirit," he writes, "that confesses that Jesus Christ is come in the flesh is of God" (I John 4:1-2). This means that the criterion for "spirituality" is to be found in the central Christian doctrine of the Incarnation—central because it implies and contains the entire Christian faith, all dimensions of the Christian worldview: creation, fall, redemption, God, world, man. But then, where is this true spirituality, this total vision of man, of his nature and his vocation, better revealed than in the Sacrament whose purpose is precisely to restore in man his true nature, to bestow upon him the new life by regenerating him "by Water and the Spirit"? It is in this context that the rite of the white garment, seemingly so secondary that it is not even mentioned in the manuals of Dogma and Moral Theology, acquires its true significance, reveals its sacramental meaning.

The fundamental rule of liturgical theology, a rule seldom applied in artificial "symbolic" explanations of worship, is that the true meaning of each liturgical act is revealed through context, i.e. by its place within the *ordo,* the sequence of acts constituting the *leitourgia*—that, in other terms, each rite receives its meaning and also its "power" from that which precedes it and that which follows. Thus, on the one hand, the rite of the white garment completes and seals Baptism itself, the *vesting* in the "shining garment," the "robe of light," responding to the *unvesting* of the catechumen prior to Baptism, to his nakedness as he enters the water of redemption. On the other hand, this rite *inaugurates* the second part of the liturgy of initiation: the anointment with the Holy Chrism, the bestowing on the neophyte of the gift of the Holy Spirit. And it is this double function of the rite that reveals the true content of the new life, the very content of its *newness.*

We know already that the unvesting of the catechumen before Baptism signified the rejection by him of the "old man" and the "old life," that of sin and corruption. It is indeed *sin* that revealed their nakedness to Adam and Eve and made them conceal it with vestments.[5] But why were they not ashamed of their nakedness before sin? Because they were vested in divine glory and light, in the "ineffable beauty" which is the true nature of man. It is this first garment that they lost, and they "knew that they were naked" (Gen. 3:7). But then the post-baptismal vesting in the "robe of light" signifies above all the return of man to the integrity and innocence he had in Paradise, the recovery by him of his true nature obscured and mutilated by sin. St. Ambrose compares the baptismal robe to the vestments of Christ on Mount Tabor. The Transfigured Christ reveals perfect and sinless humanity as not "naked" but vested in garments "white like snow," in the uncreated light of divine glory.[6] It is Paradise, not sin, that reveals the true nature of man; it is to Paradise and to his true nature, to his primordial vestment of glory, that man returns in Baptism.

Being thus the fulfillment of Baptism, the rite of the white garment inaugurates the next act of the liturgy of initiation. We are vested in this "shining robe" so that we may be anointed. In the early Church there was no need to explain the organic and self-evident connection between the two rites. The Church knew the three essential connotations of this double action, revealing the three fundamental dimensions of man's "high calling" in Christ—the *royal,* the *priestly,* and the *prophetic.* The linen ephod of King David (II Sam. 6:14), the sacerdotal vestments of Aaron and his sons (Exodus 28), the mantle of Elijah (II Kings 2:14); the "setting apart" of the King and the Priest through anointment, the prophetic gift as "anointment": all this is fulfilled in Christ Who "has made us kings and priests" (Rev. 1:6), "a chosen generation, a royal priesthood, a peculiar people" (I Peter 2:9), Who in the last days has poured out His Spirit on men so that they "shall prophesy" (Acts 2:18). Born again in the baptismal font, "renewed after the image of Him Who created him," restored to his "ineffable beauty," man is now ready to be "set apart" for his new and high calling in Christ. Baptized into Christ, having put on Christ, he is ready to receive the Holy Spirit, the very Spirit of Christ, the very gifts of Christ the Anointed—the King, the Priest and the Prophet—the triune content of all genuine Christian life, of all Christian "spirituality."

2. The Seal of the Gift of the Holy Spirit

Now, after the baptismal immersion and the vesting in

the white garment, the neophyte is *anointed* or, to use the language of the liturgy, *sealed* with the Holy Chrism.

No other liturgical act of the Church has provoked more theological controversies than this second sacrament of initiation; none has received a greater variety of interpretations.[7] In the West, as is well known, the Roman Church made it into "confirmation," the sacramental sanction of "adult" entrance into the life of the Church, and therefore severed its liturgical connection with Baptism.[8] As for the Protestants, they rejected its sacramental character as diminishing the self-sufficiency of Baptism.[9] These Western developments in turn influenced Orthodox "academic" theology, which, as we know already, adopted at an early date the very spirit and methods of the Western theological mind. As in many other areas, Orthodox theology in its treatment of Chrismation is mainly polemical. Thus, for example, Bishop Sylvester, one of the leading Russian dogmaticians (and in whose heavy five-volume Dogmatics only twenty-nine pages are devoted to the sacrament of the Holy Chrism), limits his entire presentation to only two points: to the defense— against the Catholics—of the liturgical connection of Chrismation with Baptism; to the defense—against the Protestants— of its sacramental "independence" from Baptism.[10]

Such polemics could be useful and even necessary if, at the same time, they revealed the positive Orthodox understanding of the second sacrament, of its unique significance in the faith and the experience of the Church. The tragedy of our own Westernized and academic theology, however, is that even when it denounces and fights Western errors, it begins by adopting the very presuppositions and the theological context which led to these errors. In the West, the controversy about "confirmation" was the result of a wider phenomenon: of that divorce between the *lex orandi,* the liturgical tradition of the Church, and theology—which we have already denounced as the "original sin" of all theological scholasticism. Instead of "receiving" the meaning of the sacraments from liturgical tradition, theologians created, so to speak, their own definitions of sacraments and then, in the light of such definitions, began to interpret the liturgy of the Church, to "squeeze" it into their own *a priori* approach.

We know already that these definitions were rooted in a particular understanding of *grace* and of *means of grace;* hence the "definition" of Chrismation as the sacrament which bestows on the newly baptized the gifts (χαρίσματα) of the Holy Spirit, i.e. grace, necessary for his Christian life—a definition given in virtually all theological manuals, Eastern as well as Western.[11] But the real question, the one that the Orthodox theologians while fighting on two fronts—the Roman and the Protestant—did not raise, is whether this very definition is a sufficient or even an adequate one. For as it stands, it clearly makes the Western "dilemma" unavoidable. Indeed, either the grace received in Baptism makes any new gift of grace superfluous (the Protestant solution), or the grace bestowed in the second sacrament is an entirely "different" grace and its bestowing, in virtue of this difference, not only can but even must be "disconnected" from Baptism (the Catholic solution). But what if this very dilemma is a wrong one, a pseudo-dilemma, the fruit of wrong presuppositions and, therefore, of inadequate definitions? This is the question Orthodox theology can and should answer. But it can do so only if it frees itself from Western sacramental "reductionism," if it returns to its own essential and genuine source: the *liturgical reality* which embodies and communicates the faith and the experience of the Church.

The liturgical evidence is clear. On the one hand, Chrismation is not only an organic part of the baptismal mystery: it is performed as the fulfillment of Baptism, just as the next act of that mystery—participation in the Eucharist—is the fulfillment of Chrismation:

And when he has put his garment on him the Priest prays thus: Blessed art Thou, O Lord Almighty . . . who hast given unto us, unworthy though we be, blessed purification through hallowed water, and divine sanctification through life-giving Chrismation; who now, also, hast been graciously pleased to regenerate thy servant that has newly received Illumination by water and the Spirit, and grantest unto him remission of sins, whether voluntary or involuntary. Do thou, the same Master, compassionate King of kings, grant also unto him the seal of the gift of thy Holy and

Almighty and Adorable Spirit, and participation in the Holy Body
and the precious Blood of thy Christ...

Even in our present liturgy, so different in many ways from
the ancient one, so impoverished in comparison with the
glorious paschal celebration of Baptism, there is no "hiatus"
of any kind, no discontinuity between the baptismal immersion, the rite of the white garment, and the anointment with
the Holy Chrism. One receives the white garment *because*
one is baptized and *in order* to be anointed.

On the other hand, however, the "sealing" with the Holy
Chrism is obviously a *new* act which, although prepared for
and made possible by Baptism, gives the liturgy of initiation a
dimension so radically new that the Church always knew
it to be another "mystery"—a gift and a sacrament distinct
from Baptism.

This newness is revealed above all in the formula pronounced by the celebrant *"as he anoints the neophyte on
the brow, and on the eyes, and the nostrils, and the lips,
and on both ears, and the breast, and the hands, and the feet,"*
as he "seals" the entire body with the precious myrrh consecrated by the Bishop saying: "The seal of the gift of the
Holy Spirit."

If the true meaning of this formula, or rather of the gift
that it reveals, is concealed from so many theologians, it is
because, conditioned as they are to their own categories of
thought, they simply do not hear what the Church *says,* they
do not see what she *does.* It is quite significant indeed that
while the sacramental formula is and has always been in the
singular, "the gift" (δωρεά), theologians when "defining"
this sacrament almost without exception speak of "gifts"
(χαρίσματα) in the plural; the sacrament, they say,
bestows on the neophyte "gifts of the Holy Spirit." To
them the two words, one in the plural and the other in the
singular, seem to be interchangeable. The whole point, however, is that, in the language and the experience of the Church,
they refer to different realities. The term χαρίσματα ("gifts
of the Holy Spirit," "spiritual gifts") is frequent in the New
Testament as well as in the early Christian tradition.[12] Indeed
the "diversities of gifts" coming from the one Spirit ("there

are diversities of gifts, but the same Spirit," I Cor. 12:4)
is one of the most fundamental, most joyful aspects of the
early experience of the Church. One can assume, therefore,
that if the specific purpose of Chrismation were the bestowing of any particular "gifts," or of "grace" necessary for
man's preservation in Christian life (which grace in fact is
bestowed in Baptism, the sacrament of regeneration and
illumination), the formula would have been in the plural.
And if it is not, it is precisely because the newness and the
radical uniqueness of this sacrament is that it bestows on
man not any particular gift or gifts of the Holy Spirit, *but
the Holy Spirit Himself as gift* (δωρεά).

The gift of the Holy Spirit, the Holy Spirit as gift! Are
we still able to comprehend the ineffable depth of this
mystery, its real theological and spiritual implications? Are
we able to understand that the *impossible uniqueness* of this
personal Pentecost is that we receive as *gift* Him Whom
Christ and only Christ has by *nature:* the Holy Spirit,
eternally bestowed by the Father upon His Son and Who,
at the Jordan, descends on Christ and on Him alone, revealing
Christ as the *Anointed,* as the beloved Son and the Saviour;
that, in other words, we receive as gift the Spirit who belongs
to Christ as *His* Spirit, Who abides in Christ as *His* Life?
But then, in this pentecostal anointment, the Holy Spirit
descends on us and abides in us as the *personal gift* of Christ
from His Father, as the gift of His Life, His Sonship, His
communion with His Father. The Spirit, says Christ in
promising Him, "will take what is mine and declare it to
you. All that the Father has is mine: therefore I said that
He will take what is mine and declare it to you" (John
16:14-15). And we receive this personal gift of Christ's
own Spirit not only because we are Christ's by faith and love,
but because this faith and love have made us desire *His* life,
to be *in Him,* and because in Baptism, having been baptized
into Christ, we have put on Christ. Christ is the Anointed
and we receive His anointment; Christ is the Son and we are
adopted as sons; Christ has the Spirit as His Life in Himself
and we are given participation in His Life.

And thus, in this unique, marvelous and truly divine

anointment, the Holy Spirit, because He is the Spirit of
Christ, gives Christ to us, and Christ, because the Holy Spirit
is His Life, gives the Spirit to us: "the Spirit of truth, the
gift of sonship, the pledge of future inheritance, the first
fruits of eternal blessings, the life-creating power, the fountain of sanctification. . ." (Prayer at the Anaphora, Liturgy
of St. Basil the Great); or, as another ancient liturgical
formula says, "the grace of our Lord Jesus Christ, the love
of God the Father, the communion of the Holy Spirit"—the
gift and the revelation to man of the Triune God Himself,
the knowledge of Him, the communion with Him as the
Kingdom of God and life eternal.

It must be clear now why the "seal of the gift of the
Holy Spirit" is both the fulfillment of Baptism and also a
new mystery taking the neophyte beyond Baptism. It fulfills
Baptism because only the man who in Christ has been restored
to his true nature, freed from the "sting of sin," reconciled
with God and God's creation, made *himself* again, can receive
this gift and be endowed with a "more perfect" calling. It is
a new mystery, however; it is "another" sacrament and another
epiphany because this gift of Christ's own Holy Spirit and
Christ's own high calling is precisely a *gift*. It does not
belong to human nature as such, even though it is in order
to receive this gift that man was created by God. Prepared for
and made possible by Baptism, which thus is fulfilled in it,
it takes man beyond Baptism, beyond "salvation": by making
him "christ" in Christ, by anointing him with the Anointment
of the Anointed One, it opens to man the door of *theosis,*
of *deification.*

Such is the meaning of this ineffable mystery, of the
seal. In the early Church the term *sphragis* (seal) had many
connotations.[13] But its essential significance, as revealed in
the anointment of the Holy Chrism, is clear: it is the *imprint*
on us of the One Who owns us; it is the *seal* that preserves
and defends in us the precious content and its fragrance;
it is the *sign* of our high and unique calling. In Christ, who
is "the seal of equal type" (σφραγίς ἰσότυπος), we belong
to the Father, are adopted as *sons.* In Christ, the true and
unique Temple, we become the *temple* of the Holy Spirit.

In Christ, who is the King, the Priest and the Prophet, we are made *kings, priests* and *prophets* and, in the words of St. John Chrysostom, "abundantly possess not one but all three of these dignities."[14]

Kings, priests and prophets! Such, however, is our alienation from the early Tradition that in our minds none of these "dignities" are associated with the vision and content of *our* Christian life, of *our* spirituality. We apply them to Christ: He is the King, the Priest and the Prophet; in our manuals of systematic theology, Christ's ministry is usually divided along these three categories: the royal, the priestly and the prophetic. But when it comes to us, to our new life—which we affirm to be Christ's life in us, ours in Christ—they are virtually ignored. In fact we ascribe kingship to Christ alone; we identify priesthood with clergy alone; and as to prophecy, we view it as an "extraordinary" gift bestowed upon a few, but certainly not as an essential dimension of Christian life and spirituality. This, of course, is the real reason why, in a way, the sacrament of the Holy Spirit has come to be seen as an "auxiliary" act either subordinated to Baptism, if not simply identified with it, or else entirely distinct from it, i.e. as "confirmation." This in turn has led to a narrow and impoverished understanding of the Church herself and of our life in her. What we must try to do then is to recover, inasmuch as possible, the real meaning of these three essential dimensions of genuine Christian "spirituality"—the royal, the priestly and the prophetic.

3. The King

Christ "has made us kings and priests unto God and His Father" (Rev. 1:6); in Him we have become a "royal priesthood" (I Pet. 2:9). The question is: what does this mean for our life in the Church, in the world, in the concrete and personal mode of our existence?

The first and essential connotation of the idea of kingship is that of *power* and *authority*—but of power and authority bestowed from *above,* given by God and manifesting His power.[15] In the Old Testament the symbol of the divine source of kingship is precisely the "anointment," which manifests the king as the bearer and the executor of divine decisions and authority. Through this anointment the king becomes the *benefactor* of those under his power, the one to whom their life is entrusted for protection, success, victory, welfare and happiness. But if this understanding and experience of the king is common to all "primitive" societies and to all "monarchies," the unique revelation of the Bible is that "kingship"—before it became the particular *mana* of particular men—belonged to *man* himself as his human calling and dignity. It is indeed *royal power* that God gives to the man He creates: He creates him in His own image, and this means in the image of the King of kings, of the One Who has all power and all authority. Hence the initial power given to man: "to subdue the earth and have *dominion* over the fish of the sea, and over the fowl of the air, and over every living thing that moves upon the earth" (Gen. 1:27-28).

Man was created as the king of creation: such then is the first and essential truth about man, the source and the foundation of Christian "spirituality." To be king, to possess the gift of kingship, belongs to his very nature. He himself is from above, for it is from above that he receives the image of God and the power to make creation into that which God wants it to be and to become. He is the bearer of divine power, the *benefactor* of the earth given to him as his kingdom, for its own benefit and fulfillment. This "anthropological maximalism" was always stressed by the Orthodox Tradition and defended against all attempts to "minimize" man, against all "anthropological minimalism" whether it came from the East or from the West. Even in his fall, even when he abdicates his kingship, he bears the marks of his initial royal dignity.

The second spiritual truth about man is that he is a *fallen king*. His fall is primarily the loss by him of his kingship. Instead of being the king of creation, he becomes its slave. And he becomes its slave because he rejects the power from above, abandons his "anointment." Rejecting the power from above, ceasing to be God's anointed, he is no longer the benefactor of creation; instead of leading it to its fulfillment, he wants to benefit from it, to have and to possess it for himself. And since neither he nor creation has life in himself, his fall inaugurates the reign of death. He becomes a mortal slave of the kingdom of death.

Hence, the third essential truth: man's redemption as king. In Christ, the Saviour and the Redeemer of the World, man is restored to his essential nature—and this means that he is made a king again. We often forget that Christ's title as King—the title which He affirms when He makes His triumphant entrance into Jerusalem and is greeted as "the King that comes in the name of the Lord," the title which He accepts when He stands before Pilate: "thou sayest that I am a king" (John 18:37)—is His human, and not only divine, title. He is the King, and He manifests Himself as King because He is the New Adam, the Perfect Man—because He restores in Himself human nature in its ineffable glory and power.

All this is revealed, manifested and fulfilled in the baptismal mystery. Regenerating man, it recreates him as king, for to be king is his very nature. In the eucharistic blessing of water—as we have said already—the entire cosmos is revealed again as God's gift to man, as man's kingdom. In the anointment with the "oil of gladness," the new life of the neophyte is announced as power and dominion. He is vested in royal garments, and it is Christ's own kingship that he receives in the "seal" of the Holy Chrism. Thus if Christian life and spirituality have their source in baptismal regeneration, and if spirituality is above all the fulfillment by man of the gift received in Baptism, then the first and essential foundation and dimension of this spirituality is established here, in this restoration of man as king. This means that it is primarily and essentially a *positive,* and not a negative, spirituality; that it stems from joy, acceptance and affirmation and not from fear, rejection and negation; that it is cosmical and doxological in its very content and orientation.

To say this is important because this *positive* spirituality has always had, and still has, as its shadow and counterpart even within Christianity, a *negative* spirituality whose ultimate

source is precisely fear and thus rejection of God's creation
as man's kingdom, a deeply rooted negation of creation's
ontological "goodness." Our time is especially receptive to
this negative spirituality, and the reasons for this are clear.
Tired and disillusioned by the chaos and confusion he himself
has brought about, crushed by his own "progress," scared by
seemingly triumphant evil, disenchanted with all theories and
explanations, depersonalized and enslaved by technology,
man instinctively looks for an escape, for a "way out" of
this hopelessly wicked world, for a spiritual haven, for a
"spirituality" that will confirm and justify him in his disgust
for the world and his fear of it, yet at the same time give
him the security and the spiritual comfort he seeks. Hence
the multiplication and the amazing success today of all kinds
of *escapist* spiritualities—Christian and non-Christian alike—
whose common and basic tonality is precisely negation,
apocalypticism, fear and a truly Manichean "disgust" for
the world.

Such "spirituality," even when it takes on Christian
appearances and is dressed in Christian terminology, is *not*
Christian spirituality; it is indeed a betrayal. Salvation can
never be an "escape," a mere negation, a self-righteous
delectation in one's own "withdrawal" from the wicked
world. Christ saves us by restoring our nature, which inescapably makes us *part* of creation and calls us to be its *kings.*
He is the Saviour *of* the world, not *from* the world. And
he saves it by making us again that which we are. But if
this is so, then the essential spiritual act—from which indeed
stems the whole of "spirituality"—does not consists in
identifying the world with evil, the essence of things with
their deviation from and betrayal of that essence, the ultimate
cause with the broken and evil effects of that cause. It
consists not simply in discerning the "good" from the "evil,"
but precisely in discerning the essential goodness of *all* that
exists and acts, however broken and subdued to evil is its
existence. "The whole world lies in wickedness" (I John
5:19), but the world is not evil. If the first spiritual temptation consists in identifying one with the other, Christian
spirituality begins with the discernment. We live, to be sure,

in a wicked world. There seems to be no limit to its wickedness, to suffering and cruelty, confusion and lie, sin and crime, injustice and tyranny. Despair and disgust seem to need no justification; they almost appear to be the marks of wisdom and moral decency. And yet, it is indeed the first fruit in us of restored *kingship* that we not only can, but spiritually speaking must, while in this wicked world, *rejoice* in its essential goodness and make this joy, this gratitude, this knowledge of creation's goodness the very foundation of our own life; that behind all deviations, all "brokenness," all evil we can *detect* the essential nature and vocation of man and of all that exists and that was given to man as his kingdom. Man *misuses* his vocation, and in this horrible misuse he mutilates himself and the world; but his vocation itself is *good*. In his dealings with the world, nature and other men, man misuses his power; but his power itself is *good*. The misuse of his creativity in art, in science, in the whole of life leads him to dark and demonic dead ends; but his creativity itself, his need for beauty and knowledge, for meaning and fulfillment, is *good*. He satisfies his spiritual thirst and hunger with poison and lies, but the thirst and hunger themselves are *good*. He worships idols, but his need to worship is *good*. He gives wrong *names* to things and misinterprets reality, but his gift for *naming* and understanding is *good*. His very passions, which ultimately destroy him and life itself, are but deviated, misused and misdirected gifts of power. And thus, mutilated and deformed, bleeding and enslaved, blind and deaf, man remains the abdicated king of creation, still the object of God's infinite love and *respect*. And to see this, to *detect* this, to rejoice in this while weeping about the fall, to render thanks for this, is indeed the essential *act* of genuine Christian spirituality, of the "new life" in us.

This act being posited, what are we to *do?* How are we to fulfill this *kingship?* This question takes us to the other dimension, or, better to say, to the very depth of the baptismal mystery: to the central place in it of Christ's Cross.

4. The Crucified King

If, in the baptismal mystery, our kingship is restored to
us, it is restored on the Cross by a Crucified King; if, at the
end of the entire history of salvation, a kingdom is "appointed
unto us" (Luke 22:29), it is declared to be "not of this
world," a Kingdom *to come.*

It is precisely at this point, when challenged with the
essential antinomy of Christ's Kingship and thus of our
new kingship in Christ, that Christian spirituality is threatened
by two mutually exclusive *reductions:* the reduction of this
restored kingship only to this world, or its reduction only
to the Kingdom to come. There are those who would gladly
subscribe to all that was said above about the "royal," positive
and cosmical inspiration of Christian spirituality yet would
deduce from this that its primary concern is with the *world,*
with the possibility given man to "develop" the world toward
its fulfillment as God's Kingdom. And there are those who,
stressing the "otherworldliness" of the Kingdom announced
and promised in the Gospel, reject as a temptation any
spirituality of "involvement" and "action," who build a solid
wall of separation between the "spiritual" and the "material."
Two visions, two options, two "spiritualities," implying in
fact two radically different understandings of the Church
herself and of "Christian life."

Both, however, are revealed by the Cross of Christ as
being precisely *reductions,* for ultimately both consist in
rejecting the Cross, in making it, in the words of St. Paul,
"of none effect" (I Cor. 1:17). Indeed, if in Christ I am
restored to kingship, yet if the Kingdom "appointed" unto me
is not "of this world," the question on which my whole life
as a Christian depends is: how can I *hold together* these
two realities, these two affirmations which apply to a monk
in the desert as much as to a Christian living in the "world"
and having a "secular" vocation? How can I love the world
which God has created and "loved so much," yet at the
same time make mine the apostolic precept "not to love the
world and the things that are in the world" (I John 2:15)?
How can I affirm Christ's Lordship over all that exists, yet

at the same time put my whole faith, hope and love in the Kingdom to come? How am I to assume my kingship and, at the same time, die to the world and have my life "hid with Christ in God" (Col. 3:3)?

On the level of human reasoning, in terms of neat logical categories, within our man-made "spiritualities," there can be no answer to this decisive question; the antinomy has no solution. This is why even our spiritual and religious options, in spite of the Christian appearances they so easily adopt, remain in fact pre-Christian or non-Christian and so frequently are *reduced* either to mere *escapism* or to mere *activism.* The only answer, always the same yet radically new to each man, comes to us from the mystery which constitutes the very depth, the very heart of Christian revelation; which—precisely because it is revealed to us only inasmuch as we accept it—can never be reduced to an idea, a prescription, a "passe partout" moral code; into which we ourselves must enter if we are to make ours its meaning and power: *the mystery of the Cross.*

The Kingship of Christ and our new kingship in Him not only cannot be understood and accepted apart from the mystery of the Cross: it is the Cross, and the Cross alone, that remains forever the only true *symbol,* i.e. both the epiphany and the gift, of that kingship, the revelation of its power and the communication of that power to us. It is the mystery of the Cross, and that mystery alone, that *holds together* the two affirmations which on the level of human reasoning cannot be reconciled: the one about man and his royal calling in God's creation, and the one about the Kingdom "not of this world." And it holds them together because it always reveals the Cross to be the way of life, the "invincible and ineffable and divine power" which fulfills faith as life and life as kingship.

How? By being, first of all, the true and the ultimate revelation of *this world* as the fallen world, whose fall, whose "wickedness" consists in the rejection by it of God and of His Kingship and thus of the true life given to it in creation. It is in the crucifixion of Christ that "this world" fully manifests itself, reveals its ultimate meaning. Golgotha

is truly a unique event, but not in the sense in which each
event, whatever its "importance," can be termed "unique":
limited to those alone who took part in it, to one moment
in time, to one point in space, and thus leaving "innocent" all
other men and the rest of the world. It is unique precisely
because it is the decisive and all-embracing expression, indeed
the fulfillment, of that rejection of God by man which,
according to Scripture, began in Paradise and which made
the world created by God into "this world," the dominion
of sin, corruption, and death—which made the "lawless"
rejection of God the very law of "this world's" existence.
The Cross therefore reveals each and every sin—committed
from the beginning and until the end of the world, in all
times, in all places, by all men regardless of whether they
lived before or after Christ, of whether they believed in Him
or not—to be the *rejection of God,* the acceptance of and
the surrender to the very *reality of Evil,* whose ultimate
expression is the rejection and crucifixion of Christ. If, in
the words of St. Paul, those who after the Crucifixion "fall
away from Christ crucify to themselves the Son of God
afresh" (Heb. 6:6), if, in those of Pascal, "Christ is in
agony" till the end of the world, it is because the Cross
reveals the *content* of each sin as the rejection of God, and
this rejection as the lawless law of "this world."

But being the ultimate revelation of "this world" and
its "wickedness," the Cross—and this is the second dimension
of the mystery of the Cross—is therefore its decisive and
final *condemnation.* For to manifest and reveal Evil as Evil
is precisely to condemn it. By revealing "this world" as
rejection of God and thus as *sin,* by revealing it as rejection
of Life and thus as *death,* the Cross condemns it, for sin
cannot be "corrected," death cannot be "redeemed." "This
world" is condemned because by the Cross it condemns itself:
it manifests itself as a *dead end,* as having nothing to offer,
nothing to live by but the absurdity of mortal life and the
absurdity of death. Thus the Cross of Christ reveals and
signifies to "this world" its end and its death.

Now, however, we enter into the third—the joyful and
glorious—dimension of the mystery of the Cross. In revealing

"this world" to be sin and death, in condemning it to die, the Cross becomes the beginning of the Salvation of the world and the inauguration of the Kingdom of God. It saves the world by freeing it from "this world," by revealing "this world" to be not the essence or the "nature" of the world, but a "fashion" or "form" of its existence—a fashion whose "passing away" (I Cor. 7:31) is indeed inaugurated by the Cross. And it inaugurates the Kingdom of God by revealing it to be not "another world," another creation "replacing" this one, but the same creation, though liberated from the "Prince of this world," restored to its true nature and to its ultimate destiny—when "God shall be all in all" (I Cor. 15:28).

We may understand now why in the Christian faith, as embodied and communicated in the liturgical experience of the Church, the Cross is the true epiphany of Christ's glorification and enthronement as King. "Now is the Son of Man glorified, and God is glorified in Him" (John 13:31). It is with these words that the Church, at Matins of Good Friday, begins the *celebration of Pascha.* Let me stress this once more: not on Sunday but on Friday, for in the early tradition the term *Pascha* denoted not Sunday alone, as it does today, but the indivisible mystery of the *triduum paschale,* of the three days: Friday, Saturday and Sunday. And it is this unity, this inner interdependence of the Day of the Cross, the Day of the Tomb and the Day of the Resurrection, that reveals to us the victory of Christ and His enthronement as King and, therefore, the nature of the Kingship bestowed by Him on us.

In this liturgical epiphany, Friday—the day of the Crucifixion—is truly *the day of "this world,"* the day of its ultimate self-revelation, of its apparent victory and of its decisive defeat. By rejecting and condemning Christ, "this world" reveals its ultimate wickedness, reveals itself as *evil.* By removing Him "out of its way," into death, it apparently triumphs. Yet in all this it is truly and decisively defeated. As Christ stands before His judges, is condemned, mocked, insulted, nailed to the Cross, suffers and dies, it is He and He alone who triumphs; for it is His obedience, His love,

His forgiveness that are revealed as overcoming "this world,"
and it is from the very depth of His apparent defeat that
we hear the first confession of Him as King: in Pilate's
inscription on the Cross, in the cry of the dying thief, in
the "creed" of the centurion—"truly this Man is the Son
of God."

Then comes the Great and Holy Saturday, the "Blessed
Sabbath," the day of Death's apparent victory and, again, of
its radical defeat by Christ. As Death—the very law of "this
world"—seems to "swallow" Christ and thus to achieve its
universal dominion, death itself is "swallowed by victory"
(I Cor. 15:54). For the one who voluntarily surrenders
Himself to death has no death in Him and therefore destroys
it from within by that Life and Love which are the *"death of
death."*

And when on the third day God raises Him from the
dead, His life—over which "death has no more dominion"—
manifests the presence of the Kingdom of God "in the midst
of us." This indeed is what the paschal joy is about: it is in
this world that the Kingdom which is "not of this world"
is revealed, manifested, inaugurated as new life; it is this
world of ours that now, and until its final consummation in
God, resounds with the divine "Rejoice!"

Now, and only now, can we answer the question raised
at the beginning of this chapter: about the meaning of our
new kingship bestowed upon us in the sacrament of Chrismation. We can answer it because in the Cross of Christ the
content of this kingship is revealed and its power is *granted*.
The royal anointment truly makes us kings, but it is the
crucified kingship of Christ Himself—it is the Cross as kingship and kingship as Cross—that the Holy Spirit bestows
on us. The Cross, being Christ's enthronement as King, is
revealed to us as the only way to our enthronement with
Him, to our restoration as kings.

A most perfect description of this way is given by St.
Paul: "God forbid," he writes, "that I should glory save
in the Cross of our Lord Jesus Christ *by whom the world is
crucified unto me, and I unto the world*" (Gal. 6:14). These
words express a radically new and uniquely Christian view

of the world itself and of man's calling and life in it. And its newness is precisely in this: that it transcends the polarization, the reductionism, the "either/or" of all those "spiritualities" and "worldviews" which either merely *accept* or merely *reject* the world and make religion into either a "this-worldly" activism or an "other-worldly" escapism. In all such spiritualities, in all such religion, the Cross of Christ is, in the words of St. Paul, "of none effect"; there is no need for it, and it is for this reason that it remains forever, even within religion, a stumbling block for some and foolishness for others (I Cor. 1:23).

To have the world "crucified unto me" means, above all, to have in the Cross the only criterion of everything in the world, the ultimate measure of all life and action. This means, on the one hand, the *rejection* of the world as "this world," i.e. man's enslavement to sin and death, of the world as "the lust of the eyes, the lust of the flesh and the pride of life." It is the corruption and the wickedness of the world as "this world" that Christ has revealed on His Cross and that remains forever a judgment on it and its condemnation. But it is judged and condemned in the name and for the sake, not of any other world, but of its own true nature and calling, which are equally revealed by the Cross in the Son of Man's faith, love and obedience. Thus, while revealing the self-condemnation and thus the *end* of "this world," the Cross, on the other hand, makes possible the true *acceptance* of the world as God's creation, as the object of God's infinite love and care. This is the meaning of the world's "crucifixion unto me." It is the truly antinomical coexistence, interdependence and interpenetration within the Christian faith and the Christian worldview of the rejection and the acceptance of the world: rejection as the only way to acceptance, acceptance revealing the true meaning and goal of rejection.

This worldview, however, remains an antinomy, a mere "doctrine," unless "I am crucified unto the world." Only in *me*, in *my* faith, in *my* life and in *my* action can this doctrine become life and the Cross of Christ become power. For in the Christian faith the world is not an "idea," an abstract and impersonal "totality," but always the unique gift

to a unique human being: the world given to *me* by God
as my life and my vocation, my calling, my work, my responsibility. No idea, no doctrine can save the world, yet it
perishes or is saved in each man. And it is saved each time
a man accepts the Cross and his own "crucifixion unto the
world." This means a constant, never-ending effort of discernment, a truly mortal fight for the triumph in him of
his high calling. This means the constant *rejection* of the
world as "this world"—i.e. of its self-sufficiency and self-
centeredness, of its wickedness and corruption, of all that
the Scripture calls "pride"—yet also the constant *acceptance*
of the world as God's gift to us and the means of our growth
in Him and communion with Him.

"The world crucified unto me, and I unto the world."
This then is the true description and definition of our kingship, restored to us in the royal anointment, bestowed upon
us by the Holy Spirit. "All things are yours, and you are
Christ's and Christ is God's" (I Cor. 3:23). *All things:* the
world is ours again, and truly we can have dominion over
it; every human vocation—and ultimately each one is unique
because each human being is unique—is blessed and sanctified; everything save sin and evil is accepted, can and must
be made into knowledge of God and communion with Him,
reflect and express the goodness, the truth and the beauty
of the Kingdom of God. Yet paradoxical and foolish as it
always seems to the wisdom of "this world," the inner law
of this new kingship and power is exactly opposed to the
law accepted as self-evident by "this generation."

The new and truly royal power given to man by Christ
is the power to transcend and overcome the finality of this
world, its natural limitations, its closed horizons, the power
to make the world divine again, and not God "worldly." It
is the power constantly to "reject" this world as an end in
itself, a value in itself, a beauty or a meaning in itself, the
power constantly to "recreate" it as ascension to God. For
sin consists not in a mere misuse of that power, not in its
partial deviations and deficiencies, but precisely in the fact that
man loves the world for its own sake and makes even God
into a servant of it. It is not enough to believe in God and

to make this world "religious." Rather, true belief in God and true religion consists in the mysterious yet self-evident certitude that the Kingdom of God—the object of all ultimate desire, hope, love—is, has always been, shall always be "not of this world" but is the Beyond, which alone can give meaning and value to everything in the world.

Thus to restore man as *king* is not merely to equip man with some supernatural power and skills, not merely to give his worldly activity a new orientation, not merely to make him a better engineer, doctor or writer. In all this the non-believers may be, and more often than not are, more "clever" —in science, technology, medicine, etc. To restore man as king means, first of all and above everything else, to *liberate* man from all this as being the ultimate meaning and value of human existence, the only horizon of human life. And it is this *liberation* that the modern and secular man needs more than anything else; for although he knows better and better *how* to "make things work," he has by now lost any knowledge of *what* these things are, has become the slave of the idols which he himself brought into existence. It is this freedom, coming from the knowledge and the experience of the Kingdom "not of this world," that man—and our entire world— needs, and not our miserable and self-defensive offers of "involvement," not our surrender to "this world," with its passing philosophies and jargons. Only when man has had the taste of the Kingdom on his lips does everything in this world become again a sign, a promise, a thirst and hunger for God. Only when we seek "first of all" the Kingdom do we begin truly to *enjoy* the world, truly to "have dominion over it." Then all things are pure again, our vision and knowledge of them are clear, and good is our use of them. No matter what our vocation, calling or occupation is— glorious or humble, meaningful or insignificant by the standards of "this world"—it acquires a meaning, becomes a joy and a source of joy, for we begin to perceive and to experience it not in itself but in God and as a sign of His Kingdom. "For all things are yours... whether the world, or life, or death, or things present or things to come; all

are yours. And you are Christ's, and Christ is God's" (I Cor.
3:21-23).

Such is the new kingship which we receive in the royal
anointment with the Holy Chrism, the kingship of those to
whom a "kingdom is appointed" (Luke 22:29). And those
who have tasted of its joy, peace and righteousness can
overcome this world by the glorious power of the Cross,
can offer it to God and thus truly transform it. This now
takes us to the second dignity bestowed upon us in the
sacrament of the Holy Spirit: that of *priests*.

5. The Priest

The idea of the *priestly* dimension of Christian life
received in the gift of the Holy Spirit has been forgotten
even more than that of man's new kingship in Christ. And
it has been forgotten because it has been progressively
absorbed by and virtually dissolved in the old, indeed pre-
Christian, clergy-versus-laity dichotomy, whose main emphasis
is precisely on the non-priestly nature of those called laity.
By accepting this reduction to "old" categories, by rejecting
in fact the transformation and therefore the radical *newness*
in Christ of all things, of all categories and of "religion"
itself, Christian thought ended up with a false dilemma:
either the institutional priesthood excludes from the Church
any idea of the "priestly" character of all Christian as such,
or then the priestly character of the laity and indeed of the
entire Church (defined by the Apostle as "royal priesthood")
ought to exclude the institutional priesthood. Once again
purely human logics, when applied to the mystery of the
Church, resulted in a mutilation of that mystery and, in-
evitably, in a subsequent impoverishment of theology, liturgy
and piety.

As to the early Church, she firmly held and affirmed both
the institutional priesthood *in* the Church and the "royal
priesthood" *of* the Church as the two essential and complementary dimensions of her very life: *essential* as stemming
from her experience both of Christ and of His unique priest-

hood, *complementary* as revealing in their mutual correlation each other's place and significance in the life and work of the Church.[16]

What is to be rediscovered therefore is the true meaning of *Christ's Priesthood*. For only when His Priesthood began to be reduced to "clerical" categories, to be seen as the source only of "institutional" priesthood, did the progressive deterioration mentioned above make its appearance, leading to the breakdown of the early experience and tradition. We must understand that the Priesthood of Christ, just as His Kingship and, as we shall see later, His prophetic office, is rooted above all in His *human nature,* is an integral part and expression of His humanity. It is because He is the New Adam, the Perfect Man, the Restorer of man to his wholeness and totality, that Christ is King, Priest and Prophet. In theological terms, the *soteriological* meaning of these three "offices" is founded in their *ontological* character, i.e. in their belonging to the very nature of man assumed by Christ for its salvation. This means that man's nature has a priestly dimension which, because it is betrayed and lost in sin, is restored and fulfilled in Christ. Thus the first question is: what does it mean for man that he is *priest?* Only in answering this question—which implies that of the meaning for us of Christ's Priesthood—can we understand the significance, on the one hand, of the "royal priesthood" as indeed the *mode* of Christian life and, on the other hand, of the "institutional" priesthood as the essential *form* of the Church.

"Royal Priesthood"—not kingship alone and not priesthood alone, but their belonging together as the fulfillment of one in the other, the realization of the one by the other—such is the mystery of man revealed in Christ. If the property of the king is to have power and dominion, that of the priest is to offer sacrifice, i.e. to be mediator between God and creation, the "sanctifier" of life through its inclusion into the divine will and order. This double function is man's from the very beginning, but precisely as one function, in which man's natural kingship is fulfilled in priesthood, in which his natural priesthood makes him the king of creation. He has "power and dominion" over the world, but he fulfills

this power by *sanctifying* the world, by "making" it into
communion with God. Not only is his power from God and
under God, but it has God as its goal and content, as that
ultimate *good* which, as we have seen, constitutes the inner
law of all power. Therefore this power is fulfilled in *sacrifice,*
which, long before it became almost synonymous with "ex-
piation," was and still is the essential expression of man's
desire for communion with God, of creation's longing for
its fulfillment in God, and which is essentially a movement,
an act of praise, thanksgiving and union. Thus man is *king*
and *priest* by nature and calling.

The fall of man is the rejection by him of this priestly
calling, his refusal to be priest. The original sin consists in
man's choice of a non-priestly relationship with God and the
world. And perhaps no word better expresses the essence of
this new, fallen, non-priestly way of life than the one which
in our own time has had an amazingly successful career, has
truly become the very symbol of our modern culture. It is the
word *consumer.* After having glorified himself as *homo faber,*
then as *homo sapiens,* man seems to have found his ultimate
vocation as "consumer." And there are people today who
see in the defense of the "consumer's rights" a bright and
heroical vocation! Do we have to prove that this "ideal"
simply excludes the very idea of sacrifice, the priestly vocation
of man? It is indeed the sad achievement of our age—quite
honest in this—that it proudly affirms what preceding civiliza-
tions tried, however hypocritically, to conceal. But the truth
is, of course, that the "consumer" was not born in the
twentieth century. The first consumer was Adam himself.
He chose not to be priest but to approach the world as consumer: to "eat" of it, to use and to dominate it for himself,
to benefit from it but not to offer, not to sacrifice, not to
have it for God and in God. And the most tragical fruit of
that original sin is that it made religion itself into a "consumer good" meant to satisfy our "religious needs," to serve
as a security blanket or therapy, to supply us with cheap self-
righteousness and equally cheap self-centered and self-serving
"spiritualities," the self-evident supplier of all this being
the priest whose special and sacred powers are to guarantee

the usefulness of religion in a society and a culture which
otherwise do not have the slightest interest in the divine
calling of man and the whole of creation.

Needless to say, such was not and such is not the real
Christian understanding of man, of religion and of priesthood. In His Incarnation, in His self-offering to God for
the salvation of the world, Christ revealed the true—the
priestly—nature of man, and by the gift of His life to us
—in Baptism and Chrismation—He restores us to our priesthood: to the power of presenting our "bodies a living sacrifice, holy, acceptable unto God" (Rom. 12:1), of making our
whole life a "reasonable service" (Rom. 12:1), offering,
sacrifice, communion.

But then the Church, who is the gift and the presence of
this new life in the world, who therefore *is* offering, sacrifice,
and communion, is also and of necessity priestly in her totality
as the Body of Christ, and in her members as members of
the Body. She is priestly in her relationship to herself, for
her life is to offer herself to God, and she is priestly in her
relationship to the world, for her mission is to offer the
world to God and thus to sanctify it. "Thine own of Thine
own we offer unto Thee on behalf of all and for all." If
this offering stands at the very heart of the Eucharist, the
sacrament in which the Church always becomes "that which
she is," it is because it expresses and fulfills the whole life
of the Church, the very essence of man's vocation and calling
in the world.

This calling is to sanctify and to transform ourselves and
our lives, as well as the world given to each of us as our
kingdom: *Ourselves*—by constantly offering our life, our
work, our joys as well as our sufferings to God; by making
them always open to God's will and grace; by being that
which we have become in Christ, the Temple of the Holy
Spirit; by transforming our life into that which the Holy
Spirit has made it: a "liturgy," a service to God and communion with Him. *The world*—by being truly "men for the
others," not in the sense of constant involvement in social
or political affairs, to which one so often reduces Christianity
today, but by being always, everywhere and in all things

witnesses to Christ's Truth, which is the only true life, and
bearers of that sacrificial love which is the ultimate essence
and content of man's priesthood.

Finally, only in the light of this "royal priesthood" to
which we are restored and which we receive in the Sacrament
of the Holy Spirit, can we understand the real, Christian, and
therefore new meaning of the "institutional" priesthood—the
priesthood of those whom the Church from the very beginning
"set apart" and, in an unbroken continuity from the apostles,
ordained to serve as her priests, pastors and teachers. For
it is precisely in order for the Church, for all her members
and the whole of her life, to be *priestly,* to fulfill themselves
as "royal priesthood," that she needs priests. If in Christ
man's nature itself is restored to royal priesthood and thus
each human vocation, each human life can truly be "priestly,"
it is because He Himself had no other vocation, no other
life, but to announce to men the Gospel of the Kingdom,
to reveal to them the divine Truth, to bestow upon them
by His self-sacrifice forgiveness of sins, salvation and the
gift of new life. In this sense His Priesthood is truly *unique*
and *personal.* And it is on His unique and personal Priesthood and sacrifice that Christ edifies His Church. As the fruit
and the gift of His unique Priesthood and sacrifice, the
Church does not depend on anything earthly and human,
on the measure of our response, on our achievements and
growth. As gift, she is from the very beginning the fullness
of grace and truth; there is no change and no growth in her.
Christ remains forever her only Priest, Shepherd and Teacher.
And it is in order that this unique Priesthood—truly Christ's
own and thus truly unique—might always be present in the
Church and always make her "the fullness of Him that fills
all things" (Eph. 1:23), that He establishes priests in the
Church. Their priesthood is not theirs but Christ's; their
vocation is *to have no vocation* save the *personal* vocation of
Christ, to assure the presence and the power of His Priesthood in the Church, its continuity until the consummation of
all things in God. As the Father sends His Son to save the
world, the Son chooses and sends those whom He entrusts

with the continuation of His saving ministry, the power of His unique Priesthood.

The uniqueness of this vocation lies precisely in this: that it is not *one* of the human vocations but that it is truly *set apart*—not above them as power, privilege and glory, not opposed to them as "sacred" versus "profane," but as the vocation which, by making Christ's unique Priesthood present, makes all other vocations truly the fulfillment of man's royal priesthood. The Church has priests so that she may fulfill herself as "royal priesthood." Yet it is because she has priests, and in them the unique Priesthood of Christ, that she can truly be royal priesthood. It is because the priest, not of his own volition, but by the appointment and gift of the Holy Spirit, does that which Christ did and continues to do through him: preach the Gospel, fulfill the Church in the Sacraments and "feed the sheep"—because in the priest the Church remains always the same gift of the same Christ— that in all her members she can truly witness to Christ and to the saving work He accomplished in the world.

"Kings and priests. . . ." And now, finally, *prophets*. It is in this third dignity, third gift and vocation, revealed and restored in Christ and given by Him to us, that we must discover the ultimate dimension of Christian "spirituality."

6. The Prophet

In theological manuals the third "office" of Christ is called *prophetic*. Being the fulfillment of all prophecies, He is *the* Prophet. Once more, however, what we have to understand (for this the manuals of theology virtually ignore) is that together with Christ's Kingship and Priesthood, His "prophecy" is the fullness in Him of His human nature, that He is prophet because He is the full and perfect Man.

Created as king and priest, man is also called to be prophet. If in the Old Testament this title is reserved for some men only, especially called by God and endowed by Him with "extraordinary" gifts and functions, it is because in sin man has rejected and lost his "natural" gift of prophecy, has ceased to be prophet. But at the beginning, in the Garden, God spoke to Adam "in the cool of the day" (Gen. 3:8), and Adam heard His voice; thus it is proper for man to hear God's voice and to respond to it. Moreover salvation is announced as the restoration of man to his prophetic vocation: "and it shall come to pass in the last days," says God, "I will pour out my Spirit upon all flesh: and your sons and your daughters shall prophesy..." (Acts 2:17, quoting Joel 2:28).

What is prophecy? Rather than reducing it, as we usually do, to the mysterious ability to foretell the future, we must see it as the Scripture reveals it to be: the power given to man always to discern the will of God, to hear His voice and to be—in creation, in the world—the witness and the agent of Divine Wisdom. The prophet is the one who hears God and therefore can convey God's will to the world, the one who "reads" all events, all "situations" with God's eyes and therefore can refer all that is human and temporal to that which is divine and eternal—the one, in other words, for whom the world is transparent to God. And such is the true vocation of man, his true nature.

But just as he rejected his kingship and his priesthood, so man also rejected the gift of prophecy. In his pride—and sin is the fruit of pride, of "ye shall be as gods"—man thought that he could truly *know* the world and truly *possess* it without "prophecy," i.e. without God; and it is this "non-prophetic" knowledge that he has finally come to call "objective" and to see in it the only source of all truth.

Generation after generation leaves the dreams and visions of childhood for the majestic temples of this True Knowledge: the schools and universities where "doctors" and "masters"—sure to possess the only access to Truth—quickly transform men into blind worshippers of "objectivity," but in reality into blind disciples of blind teachers. Is there any need, in this second half of our tragic century, to prove that the truly fantastic accumulation of that "objective" knowledge and of "techniques" based on it, not only has not prevented our "civilization" from becoming one all-embracing *crisis*—social, political, ecological, energetic, etc.—but that it itself is more and more revealed as the main cause of that crisis? Is it still to be proved that, however much all that knowledge and all those techniques were meant (to use the favorite slogan of our age) to *liberate* us, man feels more enslaved, more lonely, lost, bewildered and despondent, than at any other period of his history? That a dark cloud of despair, a horrible feeling of a total vacuum, permeates the very air we breathe and cannot be dispelled by the superficial euphoria of our "consumer society"? That a meaningless rebellion challenges an equally meaningless establishment in the name of absurd "liberations" whose very content is terror and blood, sex and lust, hatred and fanaticism?

The sad and ironic fact is that, having denied and rejected the gift of prophecy given to him by God for the sake of true knowledge and true freedom, man has enslaved himself to a host of false "prophecies"—the first of which is precisely the belief in "objective knowledge" and its capacity to transform and save the world. Seldom before has the world been so saturated with ideologies promising the solution to all problems as it is today; seldom before have there existed so many "soteriologies" claiming to know— "scientifically" and "objectively" the cure for all evils. Truly our time is the time of *prophetic fraud*—of the pseudo-prophecy and the pseudo-prophet in "science" and "religion" alike. The more evident the failure of the rational and scientific pseudo-prophecy becomes, the stronger grows the search for an irrational, pseudo-religious pseudo-prophecy, whose unmistakable sign is the reappearance—within our technological and rational society—of such phenomena as astrology, magic, esotericism and occult interests of all kinds, all of which proves only that *prophecy*—being "natural" to man—is indestructible in him and, when destroyed in its positive, God-given essence, inescapably reappears as a fallen, dark and demonic obsession.

The restoration by Christ of man as prophet is therefore inherent in the Christian idea of salvation. The gift of prophecy that we receive in the sacrament of the Holy Spirit is not the gift of a strange and miraculous power, of a "supernatural" knowledge different from, and even opposed to, the natural one. It is not some irrational faculty superimposed on our human reason and replacing it, making a Christian into a "Nostradamus" or a religious fortune-teller. It is not the exaltation of "visions" and "dreams" as paralogical and irrational substitutes for the *logos,* as secret "revelations" and "signs" of all kinds. Perhaps the best way to define this gift is to define it precisely as the gift of that *sobriety* which in Christian ascetical literature always is posited as the first and the essential foundation of all true spirituality. And sobriety is the opposite of "pseudo-prophecy," which is always the fruit in man of an inner *disorder,* the divorce from one another of his various faculties and gifts. Sobriety is that inner *wholeness* and *integrity,* that harmony between soul and body, reason and heart, which alone can *discern* and therefore *understand* and therefore *possess* reality in its totality, *as it is,* to lead man to the only true "objectivity." Sobriety is understanding because it *discerns* first of all and in everything—in almost unconscious movements of the soul as well as in "great events"—the good and the evil, because it "sees through" evil, even when evil vests itself, as it usually does, in garments of light. Sobriety is possession because, being the openness of the whole man to God, to His will and to His presence, the constant awareness of God, it makes man capable of receiving everything as coming from God and leading to Him, or, in other words, of giving everything meaning and value.

Such then is the gift of prophecy which we receive in the holy anointment: the gift of discernment and understanding, of the true possession, in Christ and with Him, of ourselves and of our lives. To discern and to understand does not mean to *know* everything. Thus, "it is not for us to know the times or the seasons which the Father has put in His own power" (Acts 1:7), and the Church has always been very cautious in dealing with all kinds of "futuristic" prophecies, so popular with "religious" people. Neither does the gift of prophecy make us miraculous "experts" in all things. Christ Himself "increased in wisdom and stature" (Luke 2:52), and the Church has always affirmed human reason to be the highest of God-given faculties—has ruled out and condemned any exaltation of the "irrational," any contempt for knowledge, science and wisdom in all its expressions. The gift of prophecy is not above and outside of true human nature restored by Christ, but rather the essential, the *vertical* dimension of all its components, of all human gifts and vocations. In Christ the essential knowledge has been given to us: the *knowledge of Truth*—about God and man, about the world and its ultimate destiny. And it is this Truth that makes us truly *free*, capable of discernment and understanding, that endowes us with the power to be—in all conditions and situations, in all professions and vocations, in the use of all of our human gifts— always and everywhere *witnesses to Christ*, Who is the ultimate Meaning, Content and End of all that we are, of all that we do.

Thus the anointment with the Holy Chrism is our elevation to kingship, our ordination to royal priesthood, the bestowing upon us of the prophetic charisms. We receive all this because the Holy Spirit is the gift to us of Christ Himself: the King, the Priest and the Prophet. Now, however, we must go to the second aspect of the sacrament: *the Holy Spirit Himself as Christ's gift to us.* If it is Christ Whom we receive from the Holy Spirit, if His descent upon us makes us participants of Christ's life, members of His Body, coworkers in His saving work, it is the Holy Spirit Whom Christ sends to us from His Father, as the ultimate gift and the very reality of His Kingdom.

7. The Holy Spirit

Theology defines the Holy Spirit as the Third Person of the Trinity; in the Creed we confess Him as proceeding from the Father; from the Gospel we learn that He is sent by Christ to be the Comforter, to "guide us into all Truth" (John 16:13) and to unite us with Christ and the Father. We begin each liturgical service with a prayer to the Holy Spirit, invoking Him as "the Heavenly King, the Comforter, the Spirit of Truth, Who is everywhere and fills all things,

the Treasury of Blessings and the Giver of Life." St. Seraphim
of Sarov describes the whole of Christian life as "acquisition
of the Holy Spirit." St. Paul defines the Kingdom of God
as "righteousness, and peace, and joy in the Holy Spirit"
(Rom. 14:17). We call the Saints the bearers of the Holy
Spirit, and we want our life to be spiritual.

Truly the Holy Spirit is at the very heart of Divine Revelation and of Christian life. Yet in speaking of Him it is
extremely difficult to find proper words—so difficult indeed
that for many Christians the Church's teaching about Him
as *person* has lost all concrete, existential significance, and
they see Him as divine power, not as *He* or *Thou*, but rather
as a divine *It*. Even theology, while maintaining of course
the classical doctrine of the Three Divine Persons when
speaking of God, prefers—when dealing with the Church and
Christian life—to speak of *grace*, and not of a *personal*
knowledge and experience of the Holy Spirit.

But in the sacrament of anointment we receive the Holy
Spirit Himself, and not merely "grace": such has always been
the teaching of the Church. It is the Holy Spirit, and not
some divine power, that descended on the apostles on the
day of Pentecost. It is He and not "grace" that we invoke
in prayer and acquire through spiritual effort. Thus, obviously, the ultimate mystery of the Church consists in knowing
the Holy Spirit, in receiving Him, in being in communion
with *Him*. And the fulfillment of Baptism in the holy anointment is the *personal* coming and revelation to man and the
abiding in him, of the Holy Spirit Himself. But then the
real question is: what does it mean to *know* the Holy Spirit,
to *have* Him, and to *be in* Him?

The best way to answer this question is to compare the
knowledge of the Holy Spirit with that of Christ. It is self-
evident that in order to know Christ, to love Him, to accept
Him as the ultimate meaning, content and joy of my life,
I must first know something *about* Him. No one can believe
in Christ without having heard about Him and His teachings,
and it is this knowledge *about* Christ that we receive from
apostolic preaching, from the Gospel and from the Church.
But it is not an exaggeration to say that with the Holy Spirit

this sequence—knowledge *about,* then knowledge *of,* and finally communion *with*—is reversed. There is nothing we can merely know *about* the Holy Spirit. Even the testimony of those who truly knew Him and were in communion with Him means nothing to us if we have not had the same experience. What indeed can be the meaning of the words in which the Eucharistic prayer of St. Basil speaks of the Holy Spirit: "the Gift of sonship, the pledge of future inheritance, the first fruits of eternal blessings, the life-creating power, the fountain of sanctification. . ."? When a friend asked St. Seraphim to "explain" the Holy Spirit to him, the saint gave no explanation but made him share in an experience which this friend described as that of "un-wonted sweetness," "unwonted joy in all my heart," "un-wonted warmth," and "unwonted fragrance," and which *is* the experience of the Holy Spirit; for, in the words of St. Seraphim, "when the Spirit of God descends on man and overshadows him with the fullness of His outpouring, then the human soul overflows with unspeakable joy because the Spirit of God turns to joy all that He may touch."

All this means that we *know* the Holy Spirit only by His presence in us, the presence manifested above all by ineffable joy, peace and fullness. Even in ordinary human language these words—joy, peace, fullness—refer to something which is precisely *ineffable,* which by its very nature is beyond words, definitions and descriptions. They refer to those moments in life when life is *full of life,* when there is no lack of and therefore no desire for anything, and thus no anxiety, no fear, no frustration. Man always speaks of happi-ness, and indeed life *is* a pursuit of happiness, a longing for life's self-fulfillment. Thus one can say that the presence of the Holy Spirit in us is the fulfillment of true happiness. And since this happiness does not come from an identifiable and external "cause," as does our poor and fragile worldly happiness, which disappears with the disappearance of the cause that produced it, and since it does not come from anything in this world, yet results in a joy about everything, that happiness must be the fruit in us of the coming, the

presence, the abiding of Someone Who Himself *is* Life, Joy,
Peace, Beauty, Fullness, Bliss.

This Someone is the Holy Spirit. There is no *icon,* no
representation of Him, for He was not made flesh, neither
has He become man. Yet when He comes and is present in
us, everything becomes His icon and revelation, communion
with Him, knowledge of Him. For it is He Who makes life
into life, joy into joy, love into love and beauty into beauty,
and Who therefore *is* the Life of life, the Joy of joy, the
Love of love and the Beauty of beauty, Who being above and
beyond everything makes the entire creation the symbol, the
sacrament, the experience of His presence: man's encounter
with God and communion with Him. He is not "apart" or
"outside" because He is the Sanctifier of all things, yet He
reveals Himself in this "Sanctification" as being *beyond* the
world, *beyond* all that exists. Through sanctification we truly
know *Him* and not an impersonal divine *It,* although no
human words can define and therefore "isolate" into an
"object" Him Whose very revelation as Person is that He
reveals everyone and everything as unique and personal, as
"subject" and not "object," makes everything into a personal
encounter with the ineffable divine *Thou.*

As the fulfillment of His saving work Christ promised
the descent, the coming of the Holy Spirit. Christ came to
restore us to the life which we lost in sin, to give us again
life "more abundantly" (John 10:10). And the "content" of
this life and thus of the Kingdom of God is the Holy Spirit.
When He comes "on the last and great day" of Pentecost,
it is life abundant and the Kingdom of God that are truly
inaugurated, i.e. manifested and communicated to us. The
Holy Spirit, Whom Christ had from all eternity as *His* Life,
is given to us as *our* life. We remain in "this world," we
continue to share in its mortal existence; yet because we have
received the Holy Spirit, our true life is "hid with Christ in
God" (Col. 3:3) and we are *already* and *now* partakers of
God's eternal Kingdom, which for "this world" is still *to
come.*

We understand now why, when the Holy Spirit comes,
He unites us with Christ, makes us into Christ's Body, into

partakers of Christ's Kingship, Priesthood and Prophecy. For the Holy Spirit, being God's Life, is truly the Life of Christ; He is in a unique way *His* Spirit. Christ, by giving us His Life, gives us the Holy Spirit; and the Holy Spirit, by descending upon us and abiding in us, gives us Him Whose Life He is.

Such is the gift of the Holy Spirit, the meaning of our personal Pentecost in the sacrament of the holy anointment. It *seals,* i.e. makes, reveals, confirms, us as members of the Church, the Body of Christ, as citizens of the Kingdom of God, as partakers of the Holy Spirit. And by this *seal,* it truly makes us into ourselves, "ordains" each one of us to be and to become that which God from all eternity wants us to be, revealing our *true personality* and thus our only self-fulfillment.

The gift is given fully, abundantly, overwhelmingly. "God gives not the Spirit by measure" (John 3:34), and "of His fullness have all we received, and grace for grace" (John 1:16). Now it must be appropriated, truly received, made ours. And this is the goal of Christian life.

We say "Christian life" and not "spirituality" because the latter term today has become ambiguous and confusing. For many people it means some mysterious and self-contained activity, a secret which can be broken into by the study of some "spiritual techniques." Prevalent in the world today is a restless search for "spirituality" and "mysticism," yet far from everything in this search is healthy—the fruit of that spiritual sobriety which has always been the source and foundation of the truly Christian spiritual tradition. Too many self-appointed "elders" and "spiritual teachers," exploiting what may be a genuine spiritual thirst and hunger, in fact lead their followers into dangerous spiritual dead ends.

It is important therefore, at the end of this chapter, to stress once more that the very essence of Christian spirituality is that it concerns and embraces the whole life. The *new life* which St. Paul defines as "living in the Spirit and walking in the Spirit" (Gal. 5:25) is not *another* life and not a *substitute;* it is the same life given to us by God, but renewed, transformed and transfigured by the Holy Spirit. Each Christian, whatever his vocation—be he a monk in a hermitage or a man involved in the activities of the world—is called not to split his life into "spiritual" and "material," but to restore it as a *wholeness*, to sanctify the whole of it by the presence of the Holy Spirit. If St. Seraphim of Sarov is *happy* in "this world," if his earthly life ultimately becomes one bright stream of joy, if he truly "enjoys" every tree and every animal, if he greets everyone coming to him by calling him "my joy," it is because in all of this he sees and enjoys the One Who is infinitely beyond all this and yet makes all of it the experience, the joy, the fullness of His Presence.

"The fruit of the Spirit is love, joy, peace, longsuffering, gentleness, goodness, faith, meakness, temperance..." (Gal. 5:22). These are the components of true "spirituality," the aims of all true spiritual effort, the way to *holiness,* which is the ultimate goal of Christian life. And "Holy" rather than "Spirit" is the proper name of the Holy Spirit, for the Scripture also speaks of the "evil spirits." And because it is the name of the Divine Spirit, it is impossible to give it a definition in human terms. It is not synonymous with perfection and goodness, righteousness and faithfulness, although it contains and implies all of this. It is the end of all human words because it is that *Reality* itself in which all that exists finds its fulfillment.

Only "One is Holy." Yet it is *His* holiness that we have received as truly the *new* content of our life in the "anointment" with the Holy Spirit Himself; and it is by His holiness, always growing in it, that we can truly transform and transfigure—make whole and holy—the life which God has given to us.

CHAPTER IV

The Entrance into the Kingdom

1. The Procession

In earlier times Baptism and Chrismation were administered not in the church or its vestibule but in a separate building called *baptisterion*.[1] Therefore immediately after the anointment the neophytes, vested in white garments and with candles in their hands, were led by the Bishop and the clergy who assisted him in administering the sacrament to the church, where the assembled community awaited their arrival before beginning the celebration of the paschal Eucharist.

Early commentaries always present and explain this procession as an essential and integral part of the liturgy of initiation, as the final "epiphany" of its meaning.[2] And this it remains even today, in spite of all transformations and developments, in spite also of the liturgical divorce between the administration of Baptism and the celebration of Pascha. It is important, therefore, that we recover its meaning and thus restore the understanding of Baptism in its totality.

In today's liturgical practice we find a procession at the

end of the baptismal service and we find a procession at the *beginning* of the Paschal celebration. Indeed, at the very end of the baptismal rite, immediately after the anointment with the Holy Chrism, the celebrant leads the newly baptized and his sponsors in a circular procession around the baptismal font, while the congregation sings the verse from St. Paul's Epistle to the Galatians: "...as many as have been baptized into Christ, have put on Christ. Alleluia!" (Gal. 3:27). As for the paschal celebration, everyone knows that it begins with a procession: at midnight we go around the church, and it is in front of the closed door of the church that we hear the first announcement of Christ's Resurrection.

What an overwhelming majority of the faithful does not realize, however, is that initially these two processions were but one and the same procession: that the *entrance* of the newly baptized into the church, which in the early liturgical tradition inaugurated the celebration of the Resurrection, was its true *beginning* not only "chronologically" but indeed spiritually. In other terms, the "key" to the meaning of the post-baptismal procession is to be found in its connection with Pascha, in its "direction" toward the paschal Eucharist, just as the "key" to the celebration of Pascha is to be found in its "beginning" in Baptism. But, as so often has happened in the history of liturgy, once the original "key" was lost, there appeared new and, more often than not, artificial explanations of these rites.

Thus, for example, the circular procession around the baptismal font is explained as the symbol of spiritual rejoicing, or of eternity, or of an eternal veneration of the Holy Trinity, etc. As for the paschal procession, it becomes the symbolical representation of the myrrh-bearing women on their way to the Tomb. The trouble with such explanations, with this "illustrative" symbolism, is not only that they are inadequate from the "illustrative" point of view (according to the Gospel the women went to the Tomb not at midnight but "very early in the morning . . . at the rising of the sun" and found the Tomb open and not closed, etc.) but that they obscure and mutilate the very meaning of liturgy, of liturgical *acts*. Rather than being *events* in the true sense of that term, i.e. something that truly happens *to us* and to our life, means of our entrance into the reality inaugurated and given to us by Christ and the Holy Spirit, liturgical acts and rites become mere representations which remain extrinsic to us, just as the role he assumes in a play is extrinsic to an actor.

What we must do, therefore, once we have recovered the proper "key," is to decipher something that even to historians and theologians appears to be a rather "accidental" complexity, resulting from all kinds of purely historical developments and having no real significance for the Church's *lex credendi.*

The first problem obviously concerns the post-baptismal *procession* itself. In present-day liturgical practice, having ceased to be the procession to the church and into the Eucharist, it has become, in the minds of many, a simple appendix to the baptismal rite, adding nothing to the meaning of Baptism. Our first task then is to show that even in its present form the post-baptismal procession remains an essential part of the baptismal liturgy—indeed, the ultimate *epiphany* of its meaning.

"As many as have been baptized into Christ have put on Christ," sings the Church during the post-baptismal procession. And it is this same hymn which replaces the usual *Trisagion* at the paschal liturgy (as also at the liturgy of those holidays on which the early Church administered Baptism, i.e. Christmas, Epiphany and Lazarus Saturday). But in the earlier liturgical practice the *Trisagion* ("Holy God, Holy Mighty, Holy Immortal, have mercy on us") was precisely a hymn of entrance, the *introit,* the *processional* sung by the congregation as it entered the church and prepared itself for the proclamation of the Gospel and the celebration of the Eucharist. The service of the three antiphons which today precedes the so-called "little entrance" was sung, and only on certain occasions, outside the church and on the way to it, so that our "little entrance" was a real *entrance* into the church and the *Trisagion* was the hymn expressing the meaning of that entrance as the entrance into "the holy of holies."[3] The replacement on Easter Day of the *Trisagion* with the baptismal *introit,* therefore, clearly indicates that in the mind and practice of the early Church, Baptism was organically connected with the eucharistic gathering, was to find its fulfillment in the "entrance into the Church" and the celebration of the Eucharist, and that this post-baptismal procession and entrance were the inauguration of the celebration by the Church of Christ's Resurrection. This is clearly implied also in our present baptismal rite: on the one hand, the procession around the font directly precedes the reading of the Epistle and the Gospel lessons, which normally constitute the first part of the eucharistic celebration; and, on the other hand, the lessons themselves are *paschal*—the same as the ones read at the paschal liturgy of Great and Holy Saturday.

Finally, this *paschal* and *eucharistic* meaning of the post-baptismal procession is revealed in our present paschal procession. The key symbol, essential for its understanding, is that of the *closed door*. If this symbol is no longer understood and, as we have seen, is replaced with the purely illustrative symbolism of the women at the grave, it is because of the transfer, at a relatively late date, of the appellation "royal door" from the door of the church to that of the *iconostasis*. In the earlier period, however—the one during which the baptismal liturgy reached its full paschal expression—it is the main door of the church that was called "royal door," because the entire church, and not only the sanctuary, was for the faithful the symbol and the expression of the Kingdom of God. And it is the baptismal regeneration and the anointment with the Holy Spirit that *open* the door to that Kingdom, the door shut by sin and man's alienation from God. Being the gift and the experience of resurrection, Baptism is the *confirmation* of Christ's Resurrection, the only "existential" *proof* that Christ is risen indeed and communicates His risen Life to those who believe in Him. Thus it is from the newly-baptized, it is from the procession as it reaches the "closed door" that the joyful announcement and affirmation "Christ is Risen!" is received. It is this announcement, the testimony to that which has just taken place in Baptism, that *opens the door* and *inaugurates* the celebration by the Church of Christ's Resurrection. And this celebration, this unique night which, in the words of St. Gregory of Nyssa, "becomes brighter than the day," which truly is the climax, the ultimate focus, the high point of the whole life of the Church, is thus the celebration not only of an event of the past, but of the *Kingdom of God itself,* which that event has inaugurated and has made into the life and joy of the Church. Thus Baptism truly fulfills itself as *procession* to the Church and into the Eucharist: the participation in Christ's Pascha "at His table, in His Kingdom" (Luke 22:15-16, 29-30).

The second problem related to that of the post-baptismal procession is the apparently *double* celebration of the Resurrection by the Church, first on paschal eve, with its Liturgy of St. Basil, the rite of exchanging dark vestments for white ones, its paschal lectionary and the obviously paschal joy permeating it; and then at the midnight service, which includes the paschal procession, Matins, and the Liturgy of St. John Chrysostom. This double celebration, which we also find in the *ordo* of the two other baptismal feasts, Christmas and Epiphany, has never been properly explained. All explanations for it have been almost exclusively historical and even archeological, whereas the proper "key" to it is again *theological:* it lies in the Church's initial experience of Baptism as *the* paschal sacrament and of Pascha as baptismal celebration.[4]

In the early Church, as we have said several times, Baptism of catechumens took place within the context of the great paschal Vigil itself; it was an integral part of the *nox sancta*. The Vigil began in fact as the solemn conclusion of the *catechesis,* the preparation for Baptism. And this "catechetical," pre-baptismal element is still evident in the Vespers of the Great and Holy Saturday, more especially in the fifteen lessons from the Old Testament, all of which are "paradigms" not only of Resurrection but also of Baptism, or rather of *salvation* as *passage*—from slavery to freedom, from death to life, from earth into heaven. At the conclusion of this last and solemn "catechesis," the candidates for Baptism were led in procession to the *baptisterion* while the congregation continued its "vigil," its "waiting for" their return and the eucharistic fulfillment of Pascha. There was thus but one celebration including all of this: the Vigil, the administering of Baptism, the procession and, finally, the Eucharist.

It was indeed an external, i.e. historical, factor that altered this celebration, initially one and all-embracing, and made it into two services: the one which, according to the rubrics, should take place in the evening of the Great and Holy Saturday, i.e. on paschal eve, and the other which today constitutes the paschal celebration proper. This factor was the very substantial increase in the number of catechumens, an increase which followed the Christianization of the Empire and the massive conversion of its population. It became progressively more and more difficult to baptize all candidates on the same day and within one celebration. This led, on the one hand, to an increase in the number of baptismal days: it is at this time that Christmas, Epiphany, Lazarus Saturday and, for a while, even Pentecost became "baptismal feasts." This resulted, on the other hand, in an adjustment of the paschal liturgy itself, its split into two parts: the *baptismal* and the *paschal* proper.

This adjustment, made necessary by practical needs, provoked however a *theological* and truly creative deepening of the Church's liturgical consciousness. It brought into existence a new paschal *ordo* which, without any doubt, constitutes the supreme spiritual masterpiece of the Byzantine liturgical tradition, a unique liturgical "epiphany" of the whole mystery of salvation.

Indeed, rather than simply excluding Baptism from the paschal celebration and making it into a service for "baptizands" only (the solution adopted later, at the time of liturgical decadence, and which still dominates our liturgical practice), the Church gave that celebration itself a double focus, expressing the double *experience* of Pascha, the experience of Pascha as the *end* and as the *beginning:* Pascha as the end of the history of salvation, that long sequence of *passages* which prepared for and found fulfillment in the ultimate passage accomplished by Christ, and in Him by all those who believe in Him; and Pascha as truly the beginning of the new day without evening of the Kingdom of God.

It is in the evening of Holy Saturday that the Church celebrates the "Pascha of the end." That day is the seventh day, the "Blessed Sabbath," the day of rest on which the Son of God rests after having accomplished the work of salvation and re-creation. This is truly the last day of the old time, the end of the old world. And it is of this blessed end that Baptism makes us partake; it is this fulfillment of all time and of all preparation that is at the heart of this vesperal celebration. But for the Church the evening, the end of one day and one cycle, is also the announcement and thus the beginning of the next day. Celebrating the Resurrection of Christ as the end and fulfillment, the Church announces and inaugurates its celebration as beginning. For truly the midnight service is but one lasting explosion of joy, and this joy, in the words of the paschal canon, is about the "beginning of another-eternal-life," the beginning, in our life, of the Kingdom of God. Thus, by its vesperal and baptismal celebration, Pascha reveals the time and the life of the Church as being always the *epiphany* of the *end,* and by its noctural and eschatological celebration, it reveals them always as the *beginning.*

Such are the spiritual and theological connotations of the post-baptismal *procession.* In it the new life received in Baptism and sealed in the holy anointment is revealed in its dynamic, not static, essence—revealed as an end always transformed into beginning, as indeed a passage, the "passover" from "this world" into the Kingdom of God, as a "procession" toward the day without evening of God's eternity. It connects Baptism, the sacrament of regeneration, with the Eucharist, the sacrament of the Church: the sacrament which fulfills the Church as the presence and the gift in "this world" of the Kingdom of God. It is this connection that we must now try to elucidate.

2. Baptism and Eucharist

The three-fold structure of the liturgy of initiation—

Baptism, Chrismation and Eucharist—so clearly evidenced in the early liturgical tradition, has been abandoned and ignored for such a long time in theology as well as in liturgical practice that even to speak of it is considered by many as a dangerous "innovation." To do so is necessary, however, not because of some romantic and "archeological" love for the past, the desire to see it artificially "restored" (all restorations are always artificial), but because of our certitude that only within this original structure can the full meaning of Baptism be grasped and understood.

In the early tradition Baptism, Chrismation and Eucharist "belong together,"[5] form one liturgical sequence and "ordo," because each sacrament within it is fulfilled in the other in such a way that it is impossible fully to understand the meaning of one in separation and isolation from the other two. If Chrismation, as we have tried to show, fulfills Baptism, Eucharist is the fulfillment of Chrismation. Fulfillment here means not "validity," each sacrament being "valid" in its own right, but the spiritual, dynamic and existential correlation of these sacraments in the *new life* received from Christ. In Baptism we are born again of Water and the Spirit, and it is this birth which makes us *open* to the gift of the Holy Spirit, to our personal Pentecost. And finally, it is the gift of the Holy Spirit that "opens" to us access to the Church, to Christ's table in His Kingdom. We are baptized so that we may receive the Holy Spirit; we receive the Holy Spirit so that we may become living members of the Body of Christ, growing within the Church into the fullness of Christ's stature.

If many people seem not to understand this sacramental *interdependence*—if they do not understand why, for the Fathers, Eucharist was "the sacrament of all sacraments," the self-evident fulfillment of each of them—it is because, influenced by a certain theology, they do not understand the real meaning of the Eucharist for the Church and her life. For them, Eucharist is precisely one of the sacraments, one "means of grace" among many, and, like all the others, aimed at the personal sanctification of the faithful. What they do not understand is the truly unique meaning of the

Eucharist as the sacrament of the Church, i.e. the act in which and for which the Church always "becomes that which she is," manifests and fulfills herself as the Body of Christ and the Temple of the Holy Spirit, as the actualization in "this world" of the Kingdom of God. And they do not understand this because the "Westernizing," legalistic and scholastic theology which shaped modern eucharistic practice and piety long ago reduced the Eucharist to only one "reality": the change of the bread and wine into the Body and Blood of Christ, to the exclusion of all other aspects and dimensions of the sacrament. The "transubstantiation" of the elements and their distribution as communion—personal and individual—to those worthy and willing to receive it: such are the only two aspects of the Eucharist dealt with in our manuals of theology. It is no wonder then that not only is the organic connection of the Eucharist with other sacraments—and especially Baptism—virtually ignored, but that the Eucharist virtually has ceased to be that which it was for the Fathers: the "focus," the source and the fulfillment of the *entire*—and not merely the "liturgical"—life of the Church, the sacrament of the Church's self-manifestation and edification.

In the real Orthodox tradition, however—the one revealed above all in the Eucharist itself and in its liturgical *ordo*—we find an entirely different approach. Here the *metabole* itself—the change of the bread and wine into the Body and Blood of Christ—and the communion of the Holy Gifts are viewed as the fulfillment, the crowning point and the climax, of the whole eucharistic liturgy, whose meaning is precisely that it *actualizes* the Church as new creation, redeemed by Christ, reconciled with God, given access to heaven, filled with divine Glory, sanctified by the Holy Spirit, and *therefore* capable of and called to participation in divine Life, in the communion of the Body and Blood of Christ.

Clearly only such understanding and experience of the Eucharist reveals it as the self-evident and necessary fulfillment of Baptism. Baptism, we are told, *integrates* us into the Church. But if the Church's ultimate being and essence are revealed in and through the Eucharist, if Eucharist is truly *the sacrament of the Church* and not only one of the

Church's sacraments, then of necessity to enter the Church is to enter into the Eucharist, then Eucharist is indeed the fulfillment of Baptism. And the best way to understand this is to follow the newly baptized as they now *enter* the church in procession, join the body of the believers and together with them begin their participation in the eucharistic celebration.

Indeed their entrance is first of all the act of joining the gathered community, the *Church* in the first and most literal sense of the Greek word ἐκκλησία, which means assembly, gathering. Their first experience of the Church is not that of an abstraction or idea, but that of a real and concrete unity of persons who, because each one of them is united to Christ, are united to one another, constitute one family, one body, one fellowship. The Eucharist, before it is or can be anything else, is thus *gathering* or, better to say, the Church *herself* as unity in Christ. And this gathering is *sacramental* because it reveals, makes visible and "real," the invisible unity in Christ, His presence among those who believe in Him, love Him and in Him love one another; and also because this unity is truly *new unity,* the overcoming by Christ of "this world," whose *evil* is precisely alienation from God and therefore disunity, fragmentation, enmity, separation.

This new unity, as the gathering which they have joined reveals to the newly baptized, is not limited to people alone. Having left the world behind the doors of the church, they find the same world, but purified, transfigured, filled again with divine beauty and meaning—the very icon of the Kingdom of God. It is not a gathering of "escapees" from the world, bitterly enjoying their escape, feeding their hate for the world. Listen to their psalms and hymns; contemplate the transparent beauty of their icons, their movements, of the entire *celebration.* It is truly cosmical joy that permeates all this; it is the entire creation—its matter and its time, its sounds and colors, its words and its silence—that praises and worships God and in this praise becomes again *itself:* the Eucharist, the sacrament of unity, the sacrament of the new creation.

Then the Word of God: the newly baptized heard it

while yet catechumens; but now, for the first time, they hear it not from outside, as a call and a promise, as the word *about* God, but from inside, for they are "fellow citizens with the saints and of the household of God" (Eph. 2:19) and they can now live by the Word and grow in its understanding: the Eucharist revealing the Church as the sacrament of the Word.

The offering of bread and wine: life itself restored as sacrifical movement to God, a movement that unites us to Christ's perfect Sacrifice and Self-Offering, that includes in it our whole life and the life of the whole world: the Eucharist revealing the Church as the sacrament of offering.

The kiss of peace, the confession of faith: our receiving from one another that love of God which "is shed in our hearts by the Holy Spirit which is given unto us" (Rom. 5:5), our confession of that Truth which alone makes us free again, "children of the day, children of light": the Eucharist revealing the Church as unity of faith and love.

And finally the *anaphora:* the fulfillment of the Church and in her of the entire creation in one all-embracing, truly ultimate act of thanksgiving and adoration, remembrance and anticipation; the act which, summing up all life, all time, all being, takes us into eternity, makes us stand—in Christ—before the throne of God and offer to Him Christ's eternal Eucharist.

Now the Church is *at home.* By *descending* upon her, the Holy Spirit has made her *ascend* to heaven; and it is *there,* at Christ's table in His Kingdom, in the Spirit, that she *knows* the bread and wine of her offering to have truly become the Body and Blood of Christ, the participation in His deified humanity, the communion of divine and "inexhaustible" Life.

Of all this the newly baptized have been made participants and partakers. They were baptized so that having died with Christ they might partake of His Risen Life, and it is this Risen Life that the Eucharist manifests and communicates in the Church, making her members into witnesses of the things to come.

One may understand now why the progressive divorce of

Baptism from the Eucharist, theological as well as liturgical, is more than a purely external departure from the early tradition. It really mutilates both sacraments, not of course in their *given* fullness, which is not affected by our errors and shortcomings, but in our comprehension and reception of that fullness. Made into a self-contained and self-sufficient rite, Baptism is no longer experienced as truly the *entrance* into the Church, as the constant source of her life and of life in her. As for the Eucharist, it is this divorce, this "cutting off" of the Eucharist from the other sacraments, that more than anything else has been responsible for its *reduction* to the status of one service, one "means of grace" among many, its ceasing to be understood and experienced as the sacrament of the Church.

And yet even in its present form the baptismal liturgy points *beyond itself* and thus reminds us of its essential openness toward the Church. We find this "beyond," this "openness" in the scriptural lessons read immediately after the procession around the font. Both of them—the Epistle (Rom. 6:3-11) and the Gospel (Matt. 28:16-20)—are not only "explanations" of Baptism (such biblical explanations were given before Baptism, were an essential part of catechetical preparation for it) but are above all the very revelation of that "newness of life," of that new "content" of life which one receives in Baptism. The fruit of Baptism, its true fulfillment, is a new life; not simply a better, more moral or even more pious life, but a life *ontologically* different from the "old" one. And this difference, the very content of this "newness," is that it is *life with Christ:* "...if we be dead with Christ, we believe that we shall also live with Him" (Rom. 6:8). It is *His* Risen Life "unto God" that is given to us and becomes our life and our resurrection. But His Life in us, our life in Him is precisely the Church, for she has no other being, no other purpose and no other life but to be Christ in us and we in Christ. "And, lo, I am with you always, even unto the end of the world" (Matt. 28:20): this *is* the Church; and this is why the sacrament of Christ's *parousia,* of His coming and presence, the sacrament of His sharing His Risen Life with us, is truly the sacrament of the Church and truly the fulfillment of Baptism.

3. The Rites of the Eighth Day[6]

Today the last rites of the baptismal liturgy—the washing off of the Holy Chrism and the tonsure—are performed within the same celebration, immediately after the reading of the Gospel. But in the rubrics they are called *Rites of the Eighth Day;* and in the early Church, at the time when Baptism was normally still connected with Pascha, they were performed on the eighth day, i.e. on Sunday following the paschal celebration of Baptism. And although today no one seems to pay any attention to it, it is the reference to the "eighth day" that gives us the "key" to the proper understanding of these rites.[7]

In the earlier liturgical tradition, the paschal night was not the end of the baptismal liturgy. For the entire week following it, the neophytes gathered daily in the church for the so-called *mystagogia,* i.e. the post-baptismal *catechesis* centered on the explanation of the Eucharist. This explanation was not given before Baptism because, in the firm belief of the Church, only Baptism—by *illumining* the mind and the heart of man—made him capable of entering into the mystery of the Church, able to *taste* and therefore to *see.* And just as the liturgy of the *triduum paschale* developed in connection with the baptismal rites, it is this *mystagogical* week that is at the origin of our paschal Bright Week, with its unique liturgical structure—the repetition each day of the full paschal liturgy, the change each day of the "tone"—all rubrics contributing to make this unique week one continuous joyful extension of the paschal celebration itself. For—and here is the whole point—this week is not merely time for some additional teaching; it itself is part of that teaching, the "epiphany" of something essential in the meaning of Baptism and the "newness of life" received in it. And since this epiphany precisely concerns *time,* it is made possible by means of time, or rather by means of that biblical numerical symbolism of time without which it is impossible truly to grasp the liturgical experience of the early Church.

In the biblical revelation the number *seven* stands for, is the symbol of, *the world:* of the world as created by God and thus perfect, achieved, "very good"; of the world as corrupted by man's sin and having become "this world," surrendered to evil and death; of the world, finally, as the "history of salvation," as the scene and the object of God's saving work. Of all this the seventh day, the one which measures the time of the world and therefore "organizes" its life, is both the expression and the experience. As the day on which God rested from all His work and which He *blessed,* it is the day of man's rejoicing in God and in creation as communion with God. As merely an interruption of work and not its real end, a rest made necessary by the work itself, it is the very expression of man's enslavement to the world. And finally, because it reminds man of God yet reveals to him his alienation from God and his enslavement to the world, this day is the day of expectation, of man's hope for redemption and liberation, for the day *beyond* "seven," beyond the meaningless repetition of time whose only horizon is death and destruction.

This *new day* comes, is inaugurated with the Resurrection of Christ. Having fulfilled the history of salvation, having recreated in Himself man and the world, having rested on the blessed Sabbath, Christ rose again from the dead on the "first day after Sabbath." On that day a *new time* began which—though externally it remains within the "old" time of this world and is still measured by the number seven—is known by the faithful truly to be new: open to eternity, transparent to the Kingdom of God, whose presence and power and joy it manifests in "this world." In the early Church, in the writings of the Fathers and in the liturgical tradition, the *symbol* of that new time is the number *eight.* For, on the one hand, there is no such eighth day in the time of "this world," in the old time still inescapably measured by the number seven. Yet, on the other hand, it really exists in the experience of the Church, is indeed the very "focus" of that experience. From the very beginning, it was on the *first day* of the week (i.e. on the day following the seventh day) that Christians gathered as "Church" to celebrate the Eucharist. Thus, in terms of "this world," this was one of the seven days, fully belonging to the time of this world. Yet the whole meaning of that gathering, of that celebration, as we already have said, was that in it the Church experienced herself as ascending to heaven, and this means fulfilling herself beyond time, partaking at Christ's table of His eternal Kingdom. She experienced the first day of the time of "this world" as the *eighth day*—the one beyond time, beyond seven, beyond "this world"—as her participation in the "day without evening" of the Kingdom. And it is this experience— expressed first of all in the rhythm of the *Lord's Day,* the primitive Christian Sunday, the day of the Church's eucharistic ascension to heaven—that shaped the entire liturgical life of the Church and, unknown, alas, to an overwhelming majority of Christians, continues to shape it.

Now we can return to Bright Week and to its significance in the baptismal liturgy. For it is precisely this experience of time that the Bright Week was meant to bestow upon the newly-baptized, and it is of this experience that the Bright Week was the "epiphany" and the gift: the experience of the new life as truly *not of this world,* the gift of the Church *in statu patriae,* in her heavenly fullness, as truly the gift of the Kingdom. Seven days: the whole of time fulfilled as eternity, having itself become one lasting Pascha, "joy and peace and righteousness in the Holy Spirit." Even today those very few who are given the joy of participation in the services of this unique week know that in this lasting Pascha they experience the ultimate essence of the Church, taste of that which "the eye has not seen, the ear has not heard . . . but which God has prepared for those who love Him."

This experience, however, *must end;* the newly-baptized *must return* into the world. For although the Church is "not of this world," it is "in this world" that Christ has established her and wants her to remain until the consummation of the world itself. Her task is to witness to Christ in the world whose salvation He is, to continue His saving work by making Him present, His Word heard, His Kingdom announced and manifested. Without ascending to heaven, without fulfilling herself as the Body of Christ and the Temple of the Holy Spirit—without, in other words, leaving "this world," where she is *in statu viae,* in pilgimage to and in expectation of the Kingdom of God—the Church would have nothing to witness to. Without returning into the world, she would not accomplish her divine mission, would cease to be Christ's work and sacrifice. Hence the double rhythm of the Church's life: that of *withdrawal* from "this world" into the "eighth day" of God's Kingdom, and that of *return* into the reality and the time of "seven days." Hence, the conclusion of the baptismal liturgy with rites expressing that return, signifying the beginning of Christian life as *mission* and *witnessing.*

These rites take place on the *eighth day* after Baptism. This means that this beginning is truly a *return,* that it is from within the ineffable depth of the paschal experience, the essential experience of the Church, that the newly-baptized are now *ordered* to return—are sent into the world. This Sunday, the first after Pascha, is called *New Sunday.* This means that the "new aeon," manifested and inaugurated at Pascha, remains mysteriously present, real, efficient in the "old" time of this world, that it is indeed the power by which the Church and her members can accomplish their task and their mission in the world. The time *after* Pascha begins, but it is permeated with the joy and light of Pascha, with power stemming from it, making it the source and the ultimate "term of reference" of all action and of life itself. It is into that time, the time made up of tension and fight between the *old*—in us, in the world and in life—and the *new,* that the newly baptized now are sent.

4. The Washing Off of the Holy Chrism

The first rite preparing the newly-baptized for that fight, revealing fight to be the content of Christian life, is the washing off of the Holy Chrism:

And on the eighth day the Baptized Person is brought again to the church for Ablution...

In the early practice, this rite was preceded by another one, *the imposition of hands by the Bishop on the head of the neophyte,* and this rite is still referred to in the first prayer of the "eighth-day" service. The new Christian is about to be sent into the world to be, as we have just said, a witness (literally: a *martyr*) of Christ, a promoter of the Kingdom of God and therefore a fighter against the "Prince of this World." His life will be that of constant danger and endless temptations. For we know from the Gospel that the Enemy, defeated as he is by Christ's victory, is staging an ultimate and desperate battle against those whom Christ has "won over" from him so as to deceive, if possible, even the elect (Mt. 24:24). The historical horizon of the Gospel is anything but optimistic, totally alien to our modern myth of progress: "...when the Son of man comes, shall he find faith on the earth?" (Lk. 18:8). The ultimate outcome of the fight is either eternal life or eternal death, salvation or damnation. Hence the "military" language and symbolism of the early Church, so totally alien to the "modern" Christian, obsessed as he is with "problems." It would be interesting to follow that progressive transformation of Christian mentality, the abandonment by it of its initial virility. The fact is that while the early Church understood herself as *militia Christi,* as the people of God mobilized to fight the Enemy, the modern Christian prefers to identify himself and his faith in terms of therapeutics, to see himself not as a warrior recruited for a long war but as a patient in a clinic.

To understand the rites of the "eighth day," however, one must recover the initial "military" spirit of the Church. It is indeed as a general who assumes the command of new recruits that the Bishop now faces the newly-baptized. They still wear their new and bright uniforms, they are full of enthusiasm, eager to fight and to prove themselves. But the general knows that the battle is to be a long and terrible one, that what awaits his men is suffering and fatigue and sometimes demoralization and defeat. Thus, the first prayer read

by the celebrant is a prayer asking for protection, help,
courage, faithfulness, endurance:

> ...Maintain the shield of their faith unassailed by the enemy...
> Preserve pure and unpolluted the garment of incorruption wherewith
> Thou hast endued them...

Then he lays his hand on their heads and says:

> ...Lay Thine almighty hand upon them and preserve them by the
> power of Thy goodness. Maintain unassailed the earnest of the
> Spirit, and make them worthy of life everlasting and of Thy favor...

God alone can preserve us in the predicaments and
despair of our earthly pilgrimage and fight. This laying on
of hands is thus the "commissioning" of new officers, the
receiving by them of their "marching orders," the sign and
the gift of that heroism without which there can be no Christian life.

The new Christian accepts this commission: "Bow your
heads unto the Lord..." says the celebrant, and by bowing
his head the newly-baptized signifies his obedience, his
readiness to accept the discipline of the *militia Christi,* to
remain in the ranks, to seek not his own glory and satis-
faction but the victory of His Lord.

And the celebrant prays:

> They who have put on Thee, O Christ our God, bow also their
> heads with us, unto Thee. Keep them ever warriors invincible in
> every attack of those who assail them and us; and make us all
> victors, even unto the end, through Thy crown incorruptible.
> For Thine it is to show mercy and to save us...

Now the external signs and symbols can be removed
because from now on nothing that is merely external will
be of any help; only the inner appropriation by man of the
gift of grace, faith and faithfulness will sustain him. When
the real fight begins the bright and colorful uniform is of no
use and is replaced with battle fatigues. Thus the white
garment is removed. To overcome the Enemy, Christ Himself
put aside His glorious apparel, took upon Himself the form
of a servant. Yet nowhere was His glory made more manifest
than when "He humbled Himself, and took upon Himself

the form of a servant... and became obedient unto death, even the death of the Cross" (Phil. 2:8-9). Then was the Son of Man glorified. The white garment is removed and the Holy Chrism is washed off, for they were given to be not signs but *reality itself,* to be transformed into life. This is why the celebrant, while he washes off the Chrism from the *body,* addresses the man himself:

> *Thou* art justified, *thou* art illumined, *thou* art sanctified, *thou* art washed in the Name of our Lord Jesus Christ, and by the Spirit of our God....[8]

Now the neophyte is ready to face the challenge of the world, to begin his *martyria.*

5. The Tonsure[9]

The last rite is that of tonsure. Tonsure has always been one of the fundamental religious rites: the symbol of obedience and sacrifice. From time immemorial men experienced hair as having a "mana," as the focus in man of his power and strength. An example of this belief is the biblical story of Samson. But even today something of that belief remains in man's constant preoccupation with his hair and "hairdo." It remains the expression, the symbol of man's beauty as precisely "power," the symbol of national identity (cf. the "Afro" hair style), the symbol even of some deep and pathological deviations in man. In short, there exists a "mystery of hair" as one of the fundamental means of self-expression, self-affirmation, and identity. Therefore the Christian rite of tonsure (which besides the baptismal liturgy is found in monastic tonsure and in the "setting apart" of Readers, i.e. members of the "clergy") should not be viewed as one of the many other "ancient and venerable" rites performed (no one knows why) as an integral part of our "heritage." In the Church everything is always *real.* Each symbolic act is symbolic precisely because it reveals Reality itself, that deepest and "ineffable" stratum of it with which we communicate by means of symbols and rites.

The post-baptismal tonsure begins with a solemn prayer that *sums up* the meaning of the sacrament: the restoration by it of man as the most perfect, most *beautiful* creature of God. It is as if the Church, having completed the work of this restoration, looks at man and has a cry of joy and jubilation: how beautiful!

> O Master Lord our God, Who hast honored man with Thine own image, and fashioned him from a soul endowed with word and a beautiful body which serves the soul . . . and hast set the head on high and endowed it with the highest senses . . . and hast covered the head with hair . . . and fitly joined together all his members that with them all he may give thanks unto Thee, the Supreme Artist . . .

Man is the image of God's ineffable glory and beauty, and to contemplate man's beauty and to rejoice in it is to render thanks to God Himself. As everything else in "this world," beauty also has been obscured, degraded, mutilated, is a "fallen" beauty. And the inclination is always simply to reject it as a demonic temptation. Such, however, is not the Church's experience of beauty. In spite of all its degradation it always remains divine, as God's mark and sign on His creature. Man is beautiful and must be restored in his beauty, must rejoice in this beauty and render thanks to God for it, as did that holy Egyptian monk whose purity of heart saw divine beauty even in a prostitute.

In our fallen world the way to divine beauty and to its restoration in man is obedience and sacrifice. And thus the new life begins by *sacrificing to God,* i.e. by surrendering to Him in joy and gratitude that which in "this world" has become the symbol of man's "fallen" beauty. Such is the meaning of the post-baptismal tonsure: it is man's first free and joyful sacrifice of himself to God. It is when a new-born child is baptized that this meaning becomes especially true and alive: indeed there is nothing yet that the child can offer to God, and so we take away from him the few scarce hairs he has! The glorious humiliation: the beginning of the only true way to real beauty, joy and fullness of life.

Now the baptismal liturgy has been accomplished and fulfilled. The "normal" life is about to begin. But how radically different from the "normality" preached to us and imposed on us by "this world" that life ought to be and can be, if Baptism remains its hidden yet real source and power! Just as the whole life of the Church stems from Pascha and takes us through Pentecost and the time "after Pentecost" to another Pascha, our whole life stemming from Baptism has been made into "passage"—the pilgrimage and the ascension toward the "day without evening" of God's eternal Kingdom. And as we proceed and fight and work, the mysterious light of that Day already illumines our way, shines everywhere, transforms everything, makes everything life in God and the way to God. It is when the baptismal liturgy is accomplished that Baptism begins to work in us.

CHAPTER V

The Churching

1. The Old and The New

Before concluding our study we must direct our attention to a series of prayers and rites which, although they are not directly connected with the baptismal liturgy proper, reveal certain essential dimensions of the baptismal mystery. These are: *The Prayers on the First Day after a Woman Has Given Birth to a Child,* the *Naming of a Child,* prescribed for the eighth day after birth, and finally the so-called *Churching* of both the mother and the child on the fortieth day.'

Today these rites are seldom performed, and many Christians, including priests and even theologians, question the very need for them. These rites, they claim, express an archaic and antiquated worldview, are an unjustified survival in the Church of primitive ideas and beliefs offensive especially to women and, more generally, to man's very nature. In them, natural phenomena are presented as "impurity," maternity itself as a sin to be forgiven and "purified," and woman as a "second-class" member of the Church. This view, however, is opposed by "traditionalists" who insist on the obligatory character of the rites under consideration, but who defend them,

131

strangely enough, for exactly the same reasons for which the "modernists" reject them. Here the liturgical life of the Church, the Church's very "worldview," is indeed accepted within the categories of the "pure" and the "impure," reduced to a network of "taboos" to be dealt with by means of various ritualistic "purifications."

Both attitudes are radically wrong. The error common to both is rooted in a misunderstanding of the *continuity* of the Church's institutions and liturgy with the institutions of the Old Testament, which indeed constitute the origin and the essential form of Christian liturgical tradition. To be properly understood, this continuity must always be seen and comprehended in the light of an equally radical and essential *discontinuity.* This means that if, on the one hand, the Church is truly in continuity with the "institutions" of the Old Testament, these institutions, as they become Christian, acquire a radically *new* meaning, are truly *renewed.* Why continuity? Because Christ came not to destroy the Law, but to fulfill it (Matt. 5:17); and therefore only in and by a constant and living reference to the "old" can we fully understand the "new" and make it ours, can we accept Christ as indeed the fulfillment. Yet it is He, it is His coming, that makes *all things new:* not *new things,* but the same ones *new,* i.e. revealed in their ultimate meaning, made into signs of the Kingdom to come. Thus "continuity" fulfills itself as discontinuity, and "discontinuity," in order to be fulfillment and "renewal," implies and posits "continuity."

Applied to the rites of "purification," this means, first of all, that the very categories of the "pure" and the "impure," which are indeed central *before* Christ, are radically transformed by Christ's coming—transformed and not simply abolished. "Unto the pure all things are pure: but unto them that are defiled and unbelieving nothing is pure" (Tit. 1:15). Without the distinction between the "pure" and the "impure"—a distinction proper to the "old" man and his "old" religion—the very notion and intuition of "purity" would not have existed and therefore could not have been revealed to man in its ultimate meaning. However once this ultimate meaning is revealed in Christ, the old distinction is revealed to be not "ontological" but "pedagogical," to be the means of leading man into the mystery of redemption. All things are pure because they all come from God, are part of the "very good" of divine creation. All things are impure because man has "deviated" them from being what God created them to be. All things are redeemed in the redemption of man by Christ; all become again "pure unto the pure," for ultimately they all have been created to be means of man's life with God, of his entrance into the Kingdom of God.

It is this essential Christian approach to the world—no longer in terms of "pure" and "impure" but in those of the "old" and the "new"—that is ignored and betrayed each time the life of the Church is reduced either to continuity only or to discontinuity only. The best way to overcome this reduction is to understand what the Church does and simply to listen to her and, rather than imposing on her one's own presuppositions and inhibitions, to receive from her the real meaning of her rites.

2. The Prayers of the First Day

The first rite consists of three prayers read by the priest on the first day at the place where a child was born. These prayers primarily concern the mother, and it is in them that some people detect either an "offense" to women or the justification of their own reduction of Church life to the "purity-versus-impurity" principle. But let us listen to the prayers themselves.

In the first and shortest one the Church asks God, "Who heals every infirmity and every weakness," to heal also this His servant "who this day has given birth to a child, and to raise her up from the bed whereon she lies." And the prayer adds: "for according to the words of the prophet David, *in sin we are conceived and we are all vile in Thy sight...*"

The second prayer begins with a reference to the birth of Christ, "Who was born of our all-pure Lady, the Theotokos and ever-virgin, Mary, and as a babe did lie in a manger, and as a little child was held in arms." Then it continues:

...Show mercy also upon this Thy servant, who today has borne this child; and forgive her sins, both voluntary and involuntary; and preserve her from every oppression of the Devil; and preserve the child which has been born of her from every spell and perplexity, from every storm of adversity, and from evil spirits, whether of the day or of the night. Keep her under Thy mighty hand and grant that she may speedily arise, and purify her from uncleanness, and heal her sickness; and vouchsafe unto her health and strength both of soul and body; and hedge her round about with bright and shining angels, and preserve her from every invasion of invisible spirits. Yea, Lord, and from infirmity and weakness, from jealousy and envy and from the evil eye; and have mercy upon her and upon the child... and purify her from bodily uncleanness, and from diverse inward troubles which assail her. And lead her forth by Thy speedy mercy, in submissiveness of her body, unto recovery. And grant that the child that has been born, of her may do reverence to the earthly temple which Thou hast prepared to glorify Thy Holy Name...

And finally in the third prayer, alongside the same themes of forgiveness and healing, we find a reference to child-bearing as fulfillment of God's initial commandment to man:

...For Thou hast said, O Lord, increase and multiply and fill the earth and possess it. For which cause also do we, Thy servants pray... and with awe do cry aloud to the Kingdom of Thy Holy Name: Look down from heaven and behold the weakness of us who are condemned; and pardon this Thy servant, and all the house wherein the child has been born, and those who have touched her, and all those who are here present...

Thus the first, if not exclusive, theme of all three prayers is a cry for *forgiveness*. "In sin we are conceived..." It is this apparent identification of conception, and therefore of sex, with sin and impurity that seems to "scandalize" the "modern man," even a Christian "modern man." But the scandal is only for those who have either forgotten or given away the Christian view of man and the Christian understanding of sex. Our time—and this more than anything else reveals its radical de-Christianization—is characterized by attempts to *liberate sex,* to free it above all from all connotations of sin, guilt and shame. Being "natural," sex is "good"; being good, it is "innocent": such is the basic equation implied in the "sexual liberation" of man. But it is precisely this equation that the Church rejects, just as she also rejects the Manichean and dualistic identification of sex with evil. According to the Christian worldview the nature of man, although it is fundamentally or "ontologically" *good*, is *fallen*, and fallen not in part, so as to leave some of man's faculties intact and innocent, but in its totality. And the uniqueness of "sex" is that, being organically connected with the highest of divine gifts to man, the gift of love, it is *therefore* the very focus of the tragical ambiguity proper to man's fallen nature. Indeed, on the one hand, not only is sex the expression of love; it itself *is* love. Yet, on the other hand, it is the expression, the very "locus" of man's surrender to animality, of the radical brokenness of man's nature and life, of the loss by him of his *wholeness*. The two "poles" and "drives" of sex—*love* and *lust*—are inextricably mixed, and it is impossible to separate and isolate them one from another. Hence the truly antinomical character of the Church's approach to sex and the impossibility of reducing that antinomy to a simple "black and white" solution.

It would be an error indeed to think that the Church, while denouncing and condemning sex as "bad" outside of marriage, simply affirms it as "good" within marriage. For the whole point is that whether "outside" or "inside," sex, inasmuch as it is *lust,* belongs entirely to "this world," the world whose "fashion passes away" and which in its present "fashion" does not inherit the Kingdom of God. And because sex is the focus, the very expression of that "lust of the flesh, lust of the eyes and the pride of life" which shapes and determines the life of "this world," sex is *under law and not under grace*. Being under law does not mean being condemned; it means being *regulated* in relation to and in the light of a total vision of life, *subordinated* to that vision, *contained* within its limits, within that *order* which for "this world" is its only protection against the dark and irrational powers of self-destruction. If sex is "prohibited" outside of marriage and "permitted" within it, it is because marriage —in spite of its own corruption in the fallen world—belongs to that higher vision, is capable of "entering" the Kingdom of God, whereas the mere gratification by man of his "natural" drives and urges, natural and "fulfilling" as it

may appear, not only does not belong to that vision but
ultimately leads to its destruction and is thus revealed as being
"against nature." Law cannot transform and redeem. It can,
however, by setting *limits* and maintaining a certain *order,*
point *beyond* itself, beyond fallen nature, to give man the
awareness of a higher vision of life and to make him desire it.
And it is precisely for this reason that the Church condemns
as truly *demonic* all those ideas and trends that, in various
combinations with one another, call for a "sexual liberation."
If "sex"—its understanding and the "value" ascribed
to it—has always been for the Church the very "touchstone"
of all human morality, it is not because of a morbid and guilt-
ridden obsession with flesh, as so many people think today.
In fact such morbidity, such obsessional boredom becomes
more and more the trademark of "liberated sex," of all
attempts to make sex and sex alone the sole "content" of
human life and human love. It is, on the contrary, because
of the Church's *knowledge* of the true nature of man and
his true calling, her knowledge also that such "liberation"
ultimately leads to man's total enslavement and thus to his
self-destruction as man.

In the eyes of the Church, all that the man "living in the
world and wearing flesh" can and must do is accept—in
humility and obedience—the *law* revealed by God which
"liberates" him, to some degree at least, from the dark and
irrational tyranny of sex—the law which makes sex into a
servant, however ambiguous, of love, and not into its master
and its only content. The law neither "sanctifies" sex nor
"curses" it. But by revealing to man the truth about sex,
about its inescapable and tragical ambiguity, it helps man to
preserve within himself the vision of his true nature and to
fight for its "wholeness" or, in other words, to seek *grace.*

Such then is the context within which we are to "hear"
and to understand the Church's dealings with the entrance
into the world of a new human being. What the three prayers
of the first day reveal is joy at that event, at the entrance of
another child of God into God's "marvellous light," yet also
—and *therefore*—sadness about the corruption of the world
by sin. It is the greatness of the gift that makes us measure

and realize the depth of man's fall. And if these prayers are, first of all, a cry for *forgiveness,* it is because only divine forgiveness—given and fulfilled in Christ and His Coming—can purify that joy, restore it to its fullness, make this beginning of life the beginning also of salvation and redemption. Once more human life is revealed in its truly divine glory and beauty yet also in its inescapable dependence on the "fallen" laws of "this world." Conception not only is not sin; it is indeed the fulfillment of the most wonderful of divine gifts: the power to give life. Yet it is "in sin" that we are conceived, for "lust" has become an inescapable element of conception. Birth-giving is joy, yet it is also "infirmity and weakness," suffering and pain. The life which begins is open to light and joy, open to eternity itself; yet how frail it is, how open to all kinds of dangers, how radically threatened by evil!

It is all this that the Church contemplates and reveals as she stands, in the person of the priest, before *this* mother and *this* child and gives them her first blessing, and thus refers this "first day" to the mystery of salvation. How can she *help* the mother whose fate in "this world" is to experience child-bearing precisely as "weakness and infirmity," as enslavement to fallen nature, if not by asking for forgiveness, the only true *healing,* the only true return to the *wholeness* broken by sin? Indeed it is not for some particular sin, for some particular "impurity," that the Church asks forgiveness, but for sins "voluntary and involuntary," i.e. for *sin* as the very reality of "this world," for impurity and pollution permeating the whole of it. And what can the Church offer her except *forgiveness,* which is always the *passage* into life redeemed by Christ, into the joy and fullness protected by "bright and shining angels"? What other gift can the Church offer her except that of revealing to her that this birth, like the birth of every child, and motherhood itself are transformed by the Church into the participation in the joy and the fullness of Mary's unique motherhood, by which salvation and joy came to the whole world? And finally, with what other greeting can the Church greet the child except this promise to introduce him into the glorification of

God's Holy Name, i.e. the knowledge of God and communion with Him, which *is* life eternal?

One must be not only in error but, above all, *small* and *petty* to find "offense" in these prayers, so full of divine love and concern for man, so full of the only genuine —because truly divine—*respect* for the human person. And rather than blindly following "this world" in its cheap rebellions—in the name of empty "rights," meaningless "dignity," and futile "happiness"—we ought to recover and to make ours again the Church's vision of life: the one revealed by her on the first day of each human life.

3.   The Naming of The Child[2]

The next dimension of that vision is revealed to us in *The Prayers at the Naming of a Child When He Receives His Name on the Eighth Day After His Birth.* If the prayers of the first day are primarily prayers for the mother, now the center of the Church's attention shifts to the child.

Let us notice first of all that, different in this from the previous rite, the prayers of the eighth day have a *liturgical form.* They begin with the usual doxology, the invocation of the Holy Spirit, the *Trisagion,* and the Lord's Prayer, and they are concluded with a liturgical dismissal. This in itself is an indication that we are now *on our way* to the Church. The first prayers were but an initial greeting, a first "encounter"; now the life that has just begun is made into a *procession* to the "earthly temple" where salvation is to be fulfilled. After that "beginning":

> O Lord, our God, we pray unto Thee and we beseech Thee, that the light of Thy countenance may be shown upon this Thy servant; and the Cross of Thine Only-Begotten Son may be graven in his heart, and in his thoughts: that he may flee from the vanity of the world and from every snare of the enemy, and may follow Thy commandments. And grant, O Lord, that Thy Holy Name may remain unrejected by him; and that he may be united, in due time, to Thy Holy Church; and that the dread sacraments of Thy Christ may be administered unto him. That, having lived according to Thy commandments, and preserved without flaw the seal, he may receive the bliss of the elect in Thy Kingdom...

The signing with the Cross and the wording of the prayer
which follows remind us of the "Prayers at the Reception of
Catechumens" of which we spoke at the beginning of our
study. Indeed it is the same rite, only transposed so as to meet
the conditions of infant Baptism. It is the rite of the Church
as she *takes possession* of the child in the name of Christ and
engraves him with the Sign of the Cross, the sign of Christ's
victory and lordship, and begins to prepare him for Baptism.

The only new element, then, is the *naming* of the child.
In the rites of the first day no name was pronounced. But
now the child is called by his name and this name is referred
to God's Holy Name: ". . . and grant, O Lord, *that Thy Holy
Name may remain unrejected by him.*" The name of a man,
by distinguishing him from all other men, identifies him as
person and affirms his uniqueness. The Incarnate Son of God
has a human name because He is fully *person* and not "man
in general," not an abstract and impersonal bearer of an
abstract human nature. Human *nature* does not exist outside
of *persons,* each of which is then a truly unique and wholy
personal mode of that nature's incarnation and fulfillment.
The rite of naming is therefore the acknowledgement by the
Church of the *uniqueness* of this particular child, of the
divine gift of "personality" to him. By referring it to God's
Holy Name, the Church reveals each name to be *holy,* i.e.
sanctified by the human name of Christ Himself. In Christ
the name of each human being is shown to be the name of
a child of God, created and destined for a *personal*
relationship with God, a personal participation in God's
eternal Kingdom, and not for dissolution in some impersonal
"nirvana." My name is the "I" which God creates by address-
ing it as "Thou" and which therefore He Himself reveals as
Person, as Holy Name, as the *Thou* of an eternal love and
communion. If for the Church, for all her Saints, for her
entire experience, Christ Himself is present in His Name
Jesus, if this Holy Name for us is presence, communion, joy,
power, it is because the name is the *sacrament* of the
person, the epiphany, the gift of its very essence.

The Name of Christ sanctifies and makes *holy* my
name, makes it the expression, the sacrament, of *my*

person in Christ for the whole of eternity. And the service of the eighth day—being the gift to me of my name in Christ and in His Holy Name—is thus the gift to me of that "personality" created by God which is to be restored in Baptism and saved for God's Kingdom.

In the past the name of each Christian was referred to as *holy name,* and from his very childhood he was taught to respect it as *holy.* From this intuition of the name's sacredness there developed the tradition of giving a child the name of a Saint, i.e. a name already "fulfilled" as holy by a Christian. This was not merely seeking the protection of a heavenly "patron"; rather it was the fruit of a living experience of the Church as "communion of Saints," of the certitude that *holiness* is the only true destiny and calling of man. In the light of this tradition, how sad and even demonic is the present *desacralization* of man's name, its reduction to all kinds of vulgar nicknames, the growing indifference to the Christian understanding of *word* in general and of *name* in particular. How wonderful it would be if we Orthodox Christians living in the West, rather than simply following this progressive degradation of the human name— and therefore of the *person* named by it—would begin the restoration of the name as *holy name:* first, by returning to the use of names sanctified by the holiness of the Saints, and then, by using them with the same love and veneration with which we invoke the unique and holy Name of Jesus.

The naming of the child takes place on the eighth day after his birth. We already know that the eighth day is the symbol of the Kingdom of God, of the heavenly reality *beyond* "this world" and of which we are made partakers in Baptism and Chrismation. Therefore it is toward these sacraments that the service of naming is aimed. It is not the old but the new and eternal life that constitutes its horizon; it is beyond "this world" that the Church looks as she greets a child created for eternity.

And because the entire history of salvation is again fulfilled each time a child is thus *committed* to Christ and to His Kingdom, the rite of naming is concluded with the *troparion* of the Feast of the Presentation into the Temple of

Christ Himself. We offer this child to God in the same manner in which, at a unique moment of time, a unique Child was offered to God. He became child so that all children may become children of God and enter the ineffable joy of God's life and God's Kingdom, so that each child may be revealed as a unique object of a unique love. It is to God that we commit him to whom Christ committed Himself from all eternity. For only in this commitment can the uniqueness of each human life find its fulfillment.

4. The Churching

Concerning the rites of the fortieth day there developed in the Church a confusion which must be eliminated if these rites are to receive their proper and, as we hope to show, essential function in the life of the Church.

Obviously at the root of this confusion there is a misunderstanding concerning the very notion of *churching*. We may ask: *who* is churched? On the one hand, we clearly have here the rite of the mother's return, after she has recovered from the "infirmity and weakness" of child-bearing, to full participation in the sacramental life of the Church; and thus it is *her churching*. On the other hand, the rite includes prayers for the child who is present but, as the very words of these prayers indicate, has not yet been baptized; and thus it is this bringing to the church of the *non-baptized* child that is referred to as *churching:*

> On the fortieth day the infant is brought to the Temple to be churched; that is to make a beginning of being taken into the church. And it is brought by the mother...

Finally, at the very end of the rite we find another *churching*. this one, however, to be performed, as the rubric clearly states, *if the child be baptized.*

The question which we must try to answer therefore is: what happened? Why this strange confusion and even contradiction so obvious even in the rubrics?

And it is brought by the mother, who, being cleansed and washed,
stands there, at the entrance, and desires to receive the Rite, after
the Baptism...

What rite? And why "after the Baptism" if, as we have just
seen, each word of it implies that it takes place *before*
Baptism?

The question may appear a difficult one, but the answer
to it is simple. What happened is that two rites—initially
totally distinct and independent from one another—became
confused with one another, and this, once more, under the
influence of a deficient theology of sacraments resulting in
a deficient understanding of the liturgy. These rites are: the
pre-baptismal churching of the mother *and* the child, and the
post-baptismal bringing of the child into the church. And
while only the first one *is,* and therefore ought properly to be
called, *churching,* it is in fact the second that "monopolized"
—improperly and for wrong reasons—that name, thus leading to the confusion described above.

We already know that the initial baptismal liturgy, aimed
primarily at adult catechumens, included no special rite of
"churching." Even today when an adult is baptized he is not
"churched," and this for an obvious reason. Baptism itself
is *churching* in the deepest and fullest meaning of this word:
the entrance and integration into the Church as the Body
of Christ, the Temple of the Holy Spirit, the participation
in the new life. Therefore what we today call "churching"—
the *post-baptismal* rite of bringing the child into the church
and, if it is a boy, even into the sanctuary—is *not* churching
and should not be so called. About its meaning we shall
speak later. What we want to stress here is that a separate
rite of *churching* appeared and developed in the Church *only*
within the context of infant baptism and precisely as a *pre-
baptismal* rite. This rite is the liturgical expression and
"signification" first of all of a *fact:* the practice, common in
the past to the entire Church, of the mother bringing
her child, even before it was baptized, into the liturgical
assembly of the Church. It is this *fact,* this practice, that the
Church "sanctioned" in the rite of churching, whose essential
meaning, therefore, concerns not only baptism but also the

Church's understanding of the *Christian family.*

Indeed the main characteristic of this rite is that in it the mother and the child are totally *united,* form so to speak *one* human reality and thus *one* object of blessing, sanctification and prayer:

> *Bending down his head to the mother, as she stands with the infant, the Priest makes the sign of the Cross over the infant; and touching its head, he says the prayer...*

But this ritual "unification" is true to *life* itself; it is the expression, above all of something *real.* The property of childhood is its total, even physiological dependence on the mother, and the property of motherhood, at least in its initial stage, is its equally total dependence on the child. Not only do they need one another, not only is the life of each "geared" to the life of the other, but they have the *same life:* the life of the one being the life of the other. We must not forget that, like the replacement of breast feeding with bottle feeding, the "baby-sitter" is a relatively recent innovation. In the past it was necessary, and therefore normal, for the mother to carry her child wherever she went, to be always *one* with it. It is as if, at the beginning of human life, at its formative stage, the mother truly expresses the *person* of the child and the child is truly the life of the mother as person.

Our modern theology, which in many ways has ceased to be *personal,* i.e. centered on the Christian experience of "person," nevertheless—and maybe as a result of this—has become utterly individualistic. It views everything in the Church—sacraments, rites, and even the Church herself—as primarily, if not exclusively, individual "means of grace," aimed at the individual, at his individual sanctification. It has lost the very categories by which to express the Church and her life as that new reality which precisely overcomes and transcends all "individualism," transforms *individuals* into *persons,* and in which men are persons only because and inasmuch as they are united to God and, in Him, to one another and to the whole of life.

Thus in our present practice, shaped by this deficient, one-sided and "individualistic" theology and ecclesiology, the

mother quite often "receives the rite" of the fortieth day
alone, as if it concerned only her and not precisely her *one-
ness* with the child, her motherhood itself, the very reality in
this world of that unity in which one person fulfills itself
by assuming and *being* the *life* of another person—as if the
only true "purification" of the mother did not consist essentially in her *bringing* her child to the Church and thus to
God.

This, however, is what the rite of the fortieth day, what
the simultaneous *churching* of the mother and the non-
baptized child, reveals to us. And by sanctioning this bringing
of the child, by making it "the beginning of its being taken
into the Church," it also reveals the Church's understanding
of the Christian family, or rather of its unique "function"
within the Church. For not any child can be thus "churched,"
but only the one born in a Christian family of Christian
parents, and this means in a family which, precisely as *family,*
belongs to the Church, is an organic unit within the family
of God. To be and to fulfill itself as family is indeed the
very essence of the Church. Mankind was created as *family,*
whose natural unity was to be fulfilled as unity with God,
as sharing by all of the same divine gift of life and love.
Therefore the first fruit of sin is presented in the Bible as
the murder of one brother by another, i.e. as the "breakdown"
of the family and the inauguration of "non-brotherly" life.
But then the redemption of man consists in his redemption
as member of a family, in the restoration of life itself as
family: ". . .all you are brothers" (Mt. 23:8).

This new family is the Church. But precisely because she
is the family of God, the Church restores the "natural"
family, which, like everything else in "this world," shares
in its fall; yet at the same time she depends for her own
fulfillment as family of God on the redeemed family of man.
The Church redeems the "natural" family by breaking its
sinful selfishness, self-centeredness and closeness; the family
itself begins to serve God, and this is expressed in the sacrament of matrimony and in this offering of the child, the
natural fruit and fulfillment of marriage, to God. Yet it is on
this redeemed family that the Church depends for her

own fulfillment as Church, because the family remains in this world the only divinely instituted and divinely sanctioned source of human life itself.

The new-born child *belongs* to the family. It has no "autonomous" existence of any kind; its life is totally shaped and determined—in the present as well as in the immediate yet truly formative, truly decisive future—by this belonging. And the family—if it is a Christian family— *belongs* to the Church, finds in the Church the source, the content and the transcendent goal of its existence as family. Therefore the child who belongs to the family, and in a most concrete biological sense to the mother, *thereby* belongs to the Church, is truly *her* child, already offered, already committed to God. By receiving his life from the mother, by being one with her, the child already receives a life sanctified by and open to grace, just as the catechumen is prepared for Baptism by "being taken into the Church" (cf. Liturgy of the Catechumens), by having even before Baptism the Church as mother and life.

All this is expressed in the prayer read by the Priest as he "bends down" to the mother and blesses the child that she holds in her arms:

> O Lord God Almighty, the Father of our Lord Jesus Christ, Who by Thy Word hast created all things. . . we pray and implore Thee: Thou hast saved this Thy servant by Thy will. Purify her, therefore, from all sin and from every uncleanness, as she now draws near unto Thy Holy Church: and make her worthy to partake uncondemned of Thy Holy Mysteries. And bless Thou the child which has been born of her... Increase him; sanctify him with good understanding. For Thou hast brought him into being, and hast shown him the physical light, and hast appointed him to be vouchsafed in due time spiritual light, and that he may be numbered among Thy chosen flock. . . .

For the woman, her churching is the return to the Temple of God's glory, from which she was separated for forty days by her "infirmity and weakness," the return to the Church as communion in Christ's Body and Blood. "Peace be to all," says the Priest, and this means that the churching takes place within the assembly of the faithful, is the woman's return to the visible unity of the Christian community. And then he reads the prayer in which he asks God to "wash away her bodily uncleanness and the stains of her soul... and make her worthy of the communion of Christ's Holy Body and Blood...."

As for the child, his churching consists in being brought to the Church, i.e. offered to God, as Christ Himself "was brought, on the fortieth day... into the Temple according to the Law, by Mary... and was borne in the arms of Simeon the Just..." It is the beginning of the child's "procession" to Baptism, as is clearly stated in the third and final prayer:

> ...Do Thou, O Lord, Who preservest children, bless this infant, together with his parents and sponsors and grant that, in due season, he may be united, through Water and the Spirit of the new birth, unto the holy flock of reason-endowed sheep, which is called by the name of Thy Christ...

But the ultimate meaning and also the joy of this rite is to be found—as the Church understands and experiences—in the light and the joy of the mystery of Mary, the Mother of Christ. As the mother stands at the entrance of the Church, holding her child in her arms, ready to offer it and thus her very motherhood to God, she faces, in fact, another Mother with another Child in her arms: the icon of the Theotokos, the very icon of Incarnation and of its acceptance by creation. And the Church, in her prayers, unites those two motherhoods, fills human motherhood with the unique joy and fullness of Mary's divine Motherhood. The Child Whom she bore, with Whom as Mother she was fully united, Who was her whole life, made her "full of grace." And now this grace fills the Church. And it is this grace—the grace of Mary, the grace of the Church—that each mother *receives* yet also *gives* as she brings her child to God.

The *churching* ends here after the fourth prayer and the usual final benediction. And in the light of what we have said about it, we now can understand the meaning of the *post-baptismal* rite to which even liturgical rubrics refer today as *churching,* but which in fact is the particular conclusion of infant Baptism, as distinct from the baptismal liturgy for adults. The latter, as we know, was "fulfilled" in the procession of the neophytes from the *baptisterion* to the church and their participation in the Eucharist. A child, however, cannot "proceed" and must be *taken* and *brought* into the church. Thus it is, in reality, the same *procession* but adapted to the conditions proper to infant Baptism:

> *The Priest takes the infant, and makes with it the sign of the Cross in front of the door of the temple saying:*
> The servant of God is churched: in the Name of the Father, and of the Son, and of the Holy Spirit. Amen.

First: the *door*. Baptism as *entrance* into the Church and, in her, into the new life of the Kingdom of God.

> *Then he bears him into the Temple, saying:*
> He enters into Thy holy house, to worship toward Thy Holy Temple.

After the entrance: the very life of the Church as praise and adoration, as "joy, peace and righteousness" of the Kingdom.

> *And going to the middle of the Temple he says:*
> In the midst of the church shall he sing praises unto Thee.

Finally: the Church herself as procession and ascension to the *Beyond* of the Kingdom, to the ultimate fulfillment of all life in God.

> *Then he bears him before the door of the Sanctuary.*

And the rite is fulfilled with the *eschatological* hymn of St. Simeon: "Lord, now lettest Thou Thy servant depart in peace... *for mine eyes have seen* Thy Salvation..." Baptism takes us into the Church; and the Church, by taking us to Christ's table, makes us—now, in this world, in this life—partakers and witnesses of the *Salvation* prepared by God and fulfilled in Christ.

Conclusion

To conclude this study is obviously to ask: what does all this mean? How can all this be experienced and practiced *today,* in a world which seems to be so radically different from the one in which the rites described here originated, developed and apparently were "at home"?

This questioning is necessary because, from the religious point of view, nothing is more harmful than to live by illusions in an artificially recreated past, seeking in "ancient, venerable and colorful rites" an escape from a prosaic and burdensome present. Such a religious attitude, quite common, in our days, openly contradicts the Christian faith, which is aimed at transforming life and not at supplying religious substitutes for life. To understand this study as an appeal simply to *restore* the past is to misunderstand it, for there is no simple restoration, nor can there ever be. Equally harmful, however, is the attitude which rejects the past simply because it is past, which, in other words, accepts at its face value modern rhetoric about the radical "revolution" in man's worldview that makes it impossible for him to "continue" in any ideas of the past. If we do not believe that the Holy Spirit guides the Church today as He guided her yesterday and shall guide her until the end of the world, that Christ is "the same yesterday, and today, and forever" (Heb. 13:8), then obviously we do not believe in the Church, and she is

149

either a precious "cultural heritage" to be preserved or an archaic past to be discarded.

If, however, we believe in the Church, then the study of her past has only one goal: to find, and to make ours again and again, that which in her teaching and life is truly *eternal,* i.e. which precisely transcends the categories of past, present and future and has the power to transform our lives in all ages and in all situations. And if our study of Baptism reveals a discrepancy between the past and the present, it also shows, we hope, that this discrepancy is not due, as so many people think today, to any radical transformation of man, to any "irrelevance" of supposedly antiquated ideas for "modern man," but is rooted in the progressive abandonment by Christians themselves of their own tradition, of the "worldview" stemming from their faith and expressed in their worship.

Is it not obvious indeed that man—in spite of all presumed radical changes in his ideas and worldviews—remains essentially the same? He faces the same problems, is challenged with the same eternal mysteries: those of birth and death, of suffering, joy, love, loneliness, and, above all, of the ultimate meaning of his life. Philosophers may have changed their terminology; in fact they debate the same questions. Science may have radically altered the external conditions of life; but it remains helpless—and today more than ever— in solving the ultimate questions of man's existence. And this essential "sameness" of man is nowhere better revealed than in his recurring "returns" to religiosity and credulity, which today include witchcraft, magic, orientalism of all shades, mysticism of all brands, and primitivism of all flavors.

Is it not also clear that the *gap* between the Church and the world is not particular to our time and to our civilization but, although in different ways and expressions, has existed always, because ultimately it is rooted in the nature of Christian faith itself? The Athenian "elite" laughed when St. Paul spoke to it about Resurrection. Greco-Roman civilization denounced Christianity as the *odium humani generis.* The Roman Empire persecuted Christianity, telling its followers: *"Non licet vos esse*—you ought not to exist!" But even within the so-called Christian world, during the golden age of an apparently Christian society and culture, anyone who made the effort truly to live his Christian faith, truly to follow Christ, was always—in some way or another—inescapably rejected by the "world." Thus just as man has remained essentially the same, the world in which we have to live and which is our life, new and different as it may appear, is the same world where the Christian Gospel always remains a scandal and a foolishness.

The tragedy, then, is not that the Church has failed to "understand" the world and to follow it in all its pseudo-metamorphoses. Rather, the tragedy lies in this: that she followed the world too much, adopting for the explanation of her faith philosophies and thoughtforms alien to it, polluting her piety with the old, pre-Christian dichotomy of the "natural" versus the "supernatural" and her worship with either legalistic or magical connotations, abandoning above all that which stood at the very heart of the early Christian faith: the experience of the Church herself as tension between the *old* and the *new,* between "this world" and the "world to come," as the presence "in the midst of us," and thus the anticipation, of the Kingdom of God.

And if in this "modern" world of ours—in which once again we Orthodox are a tiny minority, rejected and per-secuted, divided, fragmented, insecure, yet at the same time incredibly self-righteous and triumphalistic, endlessly glorify-ing the past which we ourselves have betrayed—an effort toward recovery is urgently needed, this effort must consist first of all and above all in the recovery by the Orthodox of their own *mind,* of that *experience* of the Church which is the only source of a truly Orthodox worldview and of a truly Christian life. And the source, always living and life-giving, is precisely *Baptism*—Baptism not as one isolated "means of grace" among many, about which all we have to do is to memorize the two-line definition given to it in a manual, but Baptism as that essential act by which the Church always reveals and communicates her own faith, her "experience" of man and the world, of creation, fall and redemption, of Christ and the Holy Spirit, of the new life of the new creation, as indeed the source of the whole life of the Church and of the Christian life of each one of us.

But for our experience of the Church and of Christian life to become *baptismal,* i.e. referred to the baptismal mystery as its source and nourishment, implies and presupposes that we rediscover the true meaning of Baptism—not Baptism itself, which is here with us unchanged, unaltered in its essence, nor its rites which, mutilated as they are, essentially remain the same, but their *meaning* and thus their *power* in us. And this can only be done through *education,* which—in the early Church at least—was always understood as the indivisible unity of *teaching, liturgical experience,* and *spiritual effort.* It is this *unity* that, more than anything else, we need today: doing what we believe, believing what we do, living in accordance with what we believe and with what, through "doing," is given to us as life and power.

Teaching: we have tried to show that each rite, each act of the baptismal liturgy is the embodiment, the revelation and the expression of the Church's faith, of her view of God, man and the world, so that if, on the one hand, one must know and have that faith in order to "understand" the liturgy, it is liturgy, on the other hand, that truly "fulfills" the faith, is its "existential" epiphany and also gift. Hence, from the earliest times, that correlation between teaching and worship, whose most typical and normative expression we found in the preparation of catechumens for Baptism and in the post-baptismal paschal *mystagogia.* It is this *norm* that we must reintroduce into our own "religious education," making it the "focus" and the inspiration of all our teaching. For as long as in our *teaching*—be it in theological seminaries or "Sunday Schools"—Bible, doctrine, liturgy, spirituality remain virtually isolated from one another, constitute autonomous "departments" loosely united within a formal "curriculum," not only does each one of them tend to become an intellectual abstraction, but none is able to reveal the *faith* in its living, concrete and truly existential fullness. Indeed, it was the triumph in the Orthodox Church of that broken Western "curriculum" that resulted in the progressive divorce of theology from liturgy and the subsequent transformation of theology, i.e. teaching, into an exclusively intellectual enterprise, aimed at "intellectuals" but virtually ignored by the Church. What must be done then—and Baptism here is a self-evident starting point—is to bring together teaching and the experience of the Church, as revealed and communicated in her worship, so as to make teaching the explanation of that experience and liturgy the fulfillment of faith.

This, however, requires from the liturgy that it be the genuine embodiment and expression of the Church's *lex orandi*. If even our brief study of the baptismal liturgy reveals the cosmical, ecclesiological and eschatological dimensions of our faith and of "spirituality," how can all this be truly "experienced" in our private and thoroughly trimmed "Christenings," which weaken and contradict virtually every precept, every teaching of the Fathers, the spirit as well as the letter of the liturgical tradition itself? Once more, we do not have to "reinvent" the baptismal liturgy. It is here—contained, implied in the rites themselves, crying for its restoration and purification. For even if it is obviously impossible simply to "return" to the great paschal celebration of Baptism, to the baptismal celebration of Pascha, it is still the paschal faith of the Church that is revealed and fulfilled in Baptism and that must be restored by the restoration of its organic unity with the eucharistic ascension—in unity with the entire Church—to Christ's table in His Kingdom. When will the Orthodox—and first of all those among them who are entrusted with guarding the Tradition—realize that much of our "traditionalism" reflects in fact a surrender to a non-Orthodox spirit, while much of that which is denounced as "innovation" is but a thirst and hunger for Orthodoxy in the fullness of its truth and power?[1]

And, finally, it is time for us to return to the baptismal sources of true Christian spirituality, to re-evaluate—in the light of the sacrament of regeneration by Water and the Spirit—the spiritual confusion of our time and the numerous pseudo-spiritual recipes offered as its solution and cure. For like doctrine and liturgy, "spirituality" is not a separate and self-contained pursuit whose techniques it suffices to master in order to succeed in it. Ultimately it is the new life itself, stemming from the Church and thus having its source and also its criteria where the Church herself has them: in the death in Christ of the old man, in the rising again in Christ of the new life, in the gift of the Holy Spirit which makes us "kings, priests, and prophets," in the participation in the hidden, yet real, life of the "eighth day," the day without evening of the Kingdom.

Obviously none of these "recoveries"—the theological, the liturgical, the spiritual—can be instantaneous, the fruit of merely external reforms and "adjustments." We need much patient study, much pastoral concern, and much love. And above all we need a deepening of our Church consciousness, of the very *mind* of the Church, truly a thirst and hunger for "living water." But I am absolutely convinced that such recovery is not only desirable and possible, but that indeed only in it, only by a common "rediscovery" of the true meaning of Baptism, of its fullness, beauty, power and joy, can we again make our faith "the victory that overcomes the world" (I Jn. 5:4).

It is this conviction that I wished to confess, however inadequately, in this study.

Selected Bibliography

(1) The books and articles on Baptism, its institution, theological significance and liturgical development, are innumerable. For bibliographical surveys of earlier studies cf. J. Coblet, *Histoire dogmatique, liturgique et archéologique du sacrement de baptême*, 2 vols. Paris, 1881; A. Almazov, *Istoriia chinoposledovanii kreshcheniia i miropomazaniia* (*History of the Liturgies of Baptism and Chrismation*), Kazan, 1885; also articles on Baptism by J. Bellamy, G. Bareille and others in *Dictionnaire de Théologie Catholique* 2 (1923) pp. 167-355; by P. de Puniet in *Dictionnaire d'Archéologie Chrétienne et de Liturgie* 2 (1925) 251-346, 685-713; by A. Vacant in *Dictionnaire de la Bible* 1, 1433-1441; by A. d'Alès — J. Coppens in *Dictionnaire de la Bible*, Supplement 1 (1928) 852-924; and by W. Deinhardt, "Taufe," in *Lexicon für Theologie und Kirche* 9 (1937) 1007-1018.

Bibliographies of more recent works in B. Neunheuser, *Baptism and Confirmation*, tr. J. Hughes, The Herder History of Dogma, New York, 1964; Marion J. Hatchett, "An Introduction to Liturgical Studies," in *The St. Luke's Journal* (The School of Theology of the University of the South) 15.4 (1972) 19-158; J. Crehan, "Ten Years' Work on Baptism and Confirmation," in *Theological Studies* 17 (1956) 494-515; W. Flemington, "Baptism," in *The Interpreter's Dictionary of the Bible* 1 (1962) 345-53; A. Stenzel, *Die Taufe. Eine generische Erklärung der Taufliturgie*, Innsbruck, 1957; R. Béraudy, "L'Initiation chrétienne," in A. G. Martimort, *L'Eglise en Prière. Introduction à la liturgie*, Paris, 1961.

For new books and reviews cf. the periodicals *Jahrbuch für Liturgik und Hymnologie* (1955 ff.), *La Maison Dieu, Revue de Pastorale Liturgique* (1945 ff.), *Yearbook for Liturgical Studies* (Notre Dame, 1960 ff.), *Studia Liturgica* (Rotterdam, 1962 ff.).

(2) For Baptism in Scripture and in Judaeo-Christianity cf. J. Daniélou, *The Theology of Jewish Christianity*, Chicago, 1964; W.O.E. Oesterley, *The Jewish Background of the Christian Liturgy*, Oxford, 1925; F. Gavin, *The Jewish Antecedents of Christian Sacraments*, London, 1928; E. Goodenough, *Jewish Symbols in the Graeco-Roman World*, 6 vols. New York, 1953-56; O. Cullmann, *Baptism in the New Testament.* London, 1950;

155

O. Cullmann, "Les Sacrements dans l'Evangile Johannique," in *La Foi et le culte de l'Église Primitive*, Neuchâtel, 1963; A. Genge, ed., *Baptism in the New Testament: A Symposium*, Baltimore, 1964; G. R. Beasley-Murray, *Baptism in the New Testament*, London, 1962; W. R. Flemington, *The New Testament Doctrine of Baptism*, London, 1957; R. Schnackenburg, *Baptism in the Thought of St. Paul*, tr. G. R. Beasley-Murray, New York, 1964; R. Brown, "The Johannine Sacramentary," in *Liturgical Studies* 23 (1962) 183-206; F. L. Cross, *I Peter: A Paschal Liturgy*, London, 1954.

(3) The main Patristic texts on Baptism and related studies cf. G. Bareille, "Baptême d'après les Pères grecs et latins," in *Dict. Théol. Cath.* 21 (1905) 178-218; R. Bour, "Baptême dans les monuments de l'antiquité chrétienne," *Dict. Théol. Cath.* 21 (1905) 233-44; P. Palmer, ed., *Sources of Christian Theology: Sacraments and Worship* 1, Westminster, Md., 1955; J. Daniélou, *The Bible and the Liturgy*, Notre Dame, 1956; A. Benoit, *Le Baptême Chrétien au II siècle. La Théologie des Pères*, Paris, 1953; L. Duchesne, *Christian Worship: Its Origin and Development*, tr. McClure, ed. 5, London, 1949.

Patristic texts: A. Hamman, ed., *Baptism: Ancient Liturgies and Patristic Texts*, Alba, Staten Island, 1967.

The Didache (7, 9, 10, 14), ed. J. Quasten in *Florilegium Patristicum* 7, Bonn, 1935, 69-111; English tr. by J. Kleist in *Ancient Christian Writers* 6, 19-21.

St. Justin Martyr, *First Apology*, Engl. tr. by Falls in *The Fathers of the Church* 6, Washington, 1948.

Tertullian, *De Baptismo*, Lat. text in *Corpus Christianorum*, Series Latina, 1, Turnhout and Paris, 1954; Engl. tr. E. Evans, *Tertullian's Homily on Baptism*, London, 1964.

St. Hippolytus of Rome, *Traditio Apostolica*, ed. B. Botte in *Liturgiewissenschaftliche Quellen und Forschungen* 39, Münster, 1963; Engl. tr. in G. Dix, *The Treatise on the Apostolic Tradition of St. Hippolytus of Rome*, London, 1937.

Didascalia Apostolorum, ed. R. Connolly, Oxford, 1929.

Didascalia et Constitutiones Apostolorum, ed. F. Funk, Paderborn, 1905; Engl. tr. in *Library of Ante-Nicene Fathers* 7; cf. also F. E. Warren, *The Liturgy and the Ritual of the Ante-Nicene Church*, London, 1897.

St. Basil the Great, *De Baptismo*, in *Patr. Graeca* 31, 1513-1628; Engl. tr. by M. Wagner in St. Basil, *Ascetical Works, The Fathers of the Church* 9, Washington, 1950.

St. Augustine, *De catechizandis rudibus*, *Patr. Lat.* 40, 309-48; Engl. tr. by J. Christopher in *Ancient Christian Writers* 2.

Serapion of Thmuis, *Euchologion*, in Quasten, *Florilegium Patristicum* 7, Bonn, 1935; Engl. transl. and commentary by J. Wordsworth, *Bishop Serapion's Prayer Book*, ed. 2, London, 1923.

St. Cyril of Jerusalem, *Procatecheses* and *Catecheses Mystagogicae*, in Quasten, *Florilegium Patristicum* 7, Bonn, 1936; Engl. tr. and commentary by F. L. Cross, *St. Cyril of Jerusalem's Lectures on Christian Sacraments*, London, 1960.

St. Gregory of Nyssa, *De Baptismo*, *Patr. Graeca* 46, *In Canticum*

Canticorum, Patr. Graeca 44; cf. A. Hamman, *op. cit.* 127 ff. and *Nicene and Post-Nicene Fathers* 5, 518-524.

St. Gregory of Nazianzen, *Oratio* 40, *In Sanctum Baptisma, Patr. Graeca* 36, 359-425; Engl. tr. *Nicene and Post-Nicene Fathers* 7, 360-377.

St. John Chrysostom, *Catecheses*, ed. A. Wenger, in *Sources Chrétiennes* 50, Paris, 1957; Engl. tr. by P. Harkins in St. John Chrysostom, *Baptismal Instructions, Ancient Christian Writers* 31; cf. T. M. Finn, *The Liturgy of Baptism in the Baptismal Instructions of St. John Chrysostom*, Washington, 1967; and L. Mitchell, "The Baptismal Rite in Chrysostom," in *Anglican Theological Review* 43 (1961) 397-403.

St. Ambrose of Milan, *De Mysteriis, De Sacramentis*, in *Florilegium Patristicum* 7, Bonn, 1936; Engl. tr. by T. Thompson, *St. Ambrose on the Sacraments and on the Mysteries*, ed. J. H. Srawley, ed. 2, London, 1950.

Theodore of Mopsuestia, *Commentary on the Lord's Prayer and on the Sacraments of Baptism and the Eucharist*, ed. and tr. by A. Mignana in *Woodbrooke Studies* 6, Cambridge, 1933; cf. also H. Lietzmann, *Die Liturgie des Theodor v. Mopsuestia*, Berlin, 1933; and J. Quasten, "The Liturgical Mysticism of Theodore of Mopsuestia," in *Theological Studies* 15 (1954) 431-9.

Ps.-Dionysius the Areopagite, *De ecclesiastica hierarchia*, in *Florilegium Patristicum* 7, Bonn, 1935; Engl. tr. by J. Parker, *The Writings of Dionysius the Areopagite*, London, 1897.

Proclus of Constantinople, *Catechesis de baptismo mystagogica*, ed. A. Wenger, in *Sources Chrétiennes* 101, Paris, 1957.

St. Maximus the Confessor, *Mystagogia, Patr. Graeca* 91; Russian tr. in *Pisaniia sviatykh Ottsov otnosiashchikhsia k istolkovaniiu pravoslavnago Bogosluzheniia (Writings of the Holy Fathers related to the explanation of Orthodox Worship)* vol. 1, St. Petersburg, 1855.

St. John of Damascus, *Expositio Fidei orthodoxae, Patr. Graeca* 94, 790-1228; Engl. tr. by F. H. Chase: *An Exact Exposition of the Orthodox Faith, The Fathers of the Church* 37, Washington, 1958.

St. Gregory Palamas: on his teaching on sacraments cf. John Meyendorff, *A Study of Gregory Palamas*, London, 1964.

Nicholas Cabasilas, *De Vita in Christo, Patr. Graeca* 150; Engl. tr. by C. J. deCatanzaro, St. Vladimir's Seminary Press, New York, 1974. Cf. also M. Lot-Borodine, *Un Maître de la spiritualité byzantine au XIV siècle. Nicolas Cabasilas*, Paris, 1958.

(4) Very few special studies in *post-patristic Orthodox theology* have been devoted to sacramental theology in general and to Baptism in particular. Cf. chapters on Baptism in manuals of dogmatic theology: C. Androutsos, Δογματικὴ τῆς ὀρθόδοξου ἀνατολικῆς Ἐκκλησίας, Athens, 1907; P. N. Trembelas, *Dogmatique de l'Église Orthodoxe Catholique*, tr. Pierre Dumont, vol. 3, Desclée de Brouwer, 1968; Makary, *Pravoslavno-Dogmaticheskoe Bogoslovie (Orthodox Dogmatic Theology)* vol. 4, St. Petersburg, 1852; Bp. Sylvester, *Opyt Pravoslavnago Dogmaticheskago Bogosloviia (Essay of Orthodox Dogmatic Theology)* vol. 4, Kiev, 1897; V. Lossky, *The Mystical Theology of the Eastern Church*, London, 1957.

On sacraments cf. C. Dyobouniotis, Τὰ μυστήρια τῆς ἀνατολικῆς ὀρθ. 'Εκκλησίας, Athens, 1912; Philaret of Moscow, *Istoriko-dogmaticheskoe obozrenie ucheniia o tainstvakh* (*Historico-dogmatical Survey of the doctrine of Sacraments*), Philaret's lectures of 1819, published as supplement to *Radost' Khristianina* (1900) 6; and (1901) 1, 10 and 11; T. Smirnov, *Proiskhozhdenie i liturgicheskhii kharakter tainstv'* (*Origin and the liturgical character of Sacraments*), in *Trudy Kievsk. Dukh. Akademii* (1874) 12 and (1875) 1; A. Katansky, *Dogmaticheskoe uchenie o semi tserkovnykh tainstvakh v tvoreniiakh drevneishikh ottsov i pisatelei tserkvi do Origena vkluchitel'no* (*The dogmatical teaching about the seven ecclesiastical sacraments in the writings of the ancient Fathers and doctors up to Origen*) St. Petersburg, 1877; M. Yastrebov, *O Tainstvakh* (*On Sacraments*), in *Trudy Kievsk. Dukh. Akad.* (1907) 1, 2; (1908) 1. N. Afanassiev, *Vstuplenie v Tserkov'* (*Entrance into the Church*), mimeographed edition, Paris, 1951.

(5)   A useful collection of the main baptismal liturgies was published by E. C. Whitaker, *Documents of the Baptismal Liturgy*, ed. 2, London, 1970; also P. F. Palmer, *Sources of Christian Theology, Sacraments and Worship* 1, Westminster, Md., 1955.

Only one rite—the "Byzantine"—is used today in all Orthodox Churches. It is derived from the Syrian liturgical tradition and is very similar to the rite described in Chrysostom's *Baptismal Instructions* (cf. Thomas M. Finn, *The Liturgy of Baptism in the Baptismal Instructions of St. John Chrysostom*, Washington, 1967). The earliest record of the Constantinopolitan rite is in the *Euchologion Barberini* (ca. A.D. 790). It was published by Conybeare and McLean, *Rituale Armenorum*, Oxford, 1905. For its development cf. A. Dimitrievsky, *Opisanie liturgicheskikh rukopisei . . . pravoslavnago Vostoka* (*Description of Liturgical MSS . . . of the Orthodox East*), vol. 2 *Eukhologia*, Kiev, 1901. Cf. Almazov, *Istoriia. . .* English translations are numerous. We use mainly, but not exclusively, that by I. F. Hapgood, *Service Book of the Holy Orthodox Catholic Apostolic Church*, 2 rev. ed., New York, 1922.

(6)   Among explanations of the baptismal rites the best known are: Symeon of Thessalonica, Περὶ τῶν ἱερῶν τελετῶν, *Patr. Graeca* 155; Russian tr. in *Pisania sviatykh Ottsov...*, vol. 2, St. Petersburg 1856; P. Robotis, Χριστιανικὴ λειτουργικὴ ὑπὸ Π. Ρομπότου, Athens, 1869; J. E. Mesoloras, 'Εγχειρίδιον λειτουργικῆς τῆς ὀρθοδόξου ἀνατολικῆς ἐκκλησίας, Athens, 1895; Archbishop Benjamin, *Novaia Skrizhal'*, ed. 1, Moscow, 1803, ed. 17, 1908; K. Nikolsky, *Posobie k izucheniiu ustava bogosluzheniia pravoslavnoi Tserkvi* (*Manual of the order of Orth. Worship*) ed. 5, St. Petersburg, 1894; A. Jhelobvsky, *Kratkoe ob"iasnenie semi tainstv' khristovykh* (*Short explanation of the seven sacraments*), St. Petersburg, 1900; Bp. Hermogen, *O Sv. Tainstvakh prav. kat. vost. tserkvi* (*On the seven sacraments of the Orthodox Catholic Eastern Church*) ed. 2, St. Petersburg, 1904.

Notes and References

INTRODUCTION
TO REDISCOVER BAPTISM

[1]On the liturgical connection between Baptism and the celebration of Pascha cf. Tertullian:

> The Passover provides the day of most solemnity for baptism, for then was accomplished our Lord's passion, and into it we are baptized... After that Pentecost is a most auspicious period for arranging baptism, for during it our Lord's Resurrection was several times made known among the disciples, and the grace of the Holy Spirit first given.... (*De Baptismo* 19).

Cf. also an early description of Easter Baptism in Jerusalem in Etheria's *Pilgrimage,* E. C. Whitaker, *op. cit.* pp. 41-44. For the Church of Constantinople, cf. Codex Barberini, fol. 260 ff, in Whitaker, p. 69 ff. At the end of the fourth century Baptism was also performed at Christmas, Epiphany and Pentecost (cf. A. Baumstark, *Comparative Liturgy,* tr. F. Cross, rev. B. Botte, Westminster, Md., 1958, pp. 158-9). It is noteworthy, however, that liturgically the celebration of Christmas and Epiphany is even today patterned after the celebration of Pascha and in the old *Typica* both feasts are referred to as "Pascha—a Three-Day Feast," "Pascha" here meaning the inclusion of Baptism into their celebration. Cf. also L. Bouyer, *The Paschal Mystery.*

[2]Cf. at Vespers of Great and Holy Saturday (vespers which was the beginning of the great paschal vigil) the baptismal character of the Old Testament readings (cf. P. Lundberg, *La typologie baptismale dans l' ancienne Église,* Uppsala, 1942, and J. Daniélou, *Bible and Liturgy,* Notre Dame, 1956); the replacement of the *Trisagion* (the old hymn of entrance or processional) by the verse: "As many as have been baptized into Christ have put on Christ, Alleluia!"; the reading as New Testament lessons of the baptismal texts: Rom. 6 and Matt. 28, etc.

[3]Cf. the manuals of dogmatics enumerated in "Selected Bibliography" above.

[4]Cf. my *Introduction to Liturgical Theology.* Faith Press, London, 1966.

CHAPTER I

PREPARATION FOR BAPTISM

[1]Cf. *The Prayers at the Reception of the Catechumens,* I. F. Hapgood, *Service Book...* 2 rev. ed. New York, 1922, pp. 271-275.

[2]Cf. my *Great Lent,* St. Vladimir's Seminary Press, New York, 1969, rev. ed. 1974, pp. 14, 137. On the institution of the *catechumenate* cf. H. Leclercq, "Catéchèse, catéchisme, catéchumène," in *Dictionnaire d'Archéologie Chrétienne et de Liturgie* 2, 2 (1910) 2530-79; J. Daniélou, "L'institution catéchumenale aux premiers siècles," in *Documentation catéchistique* (Commission nationale de l'enseignement religieux), Dijon, 1957, pp. 27-36. Also *La Maison Dieu* 10 (1947): "L'initiation chrétienne," and 58 (1959): "Du catéchumènat à la confirmation."

[3]On liturgy as "preparation and fulfillment" cf. my *Great Lent,* pp. 45-55.

[4]The institution of *sponsors* having become virtually a nominal one, it is important to understand its meaning and function in the past as well as its possible, and in my opinion essential, use today. The sponsors are already mentioned in the *Apostolic Tradition,* 15:

> ...and let them (candidates for Baptism) be examined about the reason why they have come forward to the faith. And *those who bring them* shall bear witness for them, whether they are able to hear (the word). Let their life and manner of living be inquired into...

Fr. Finn, in his book on *The Liturgy of Baptism in the Baptismal Instructions of St. John Chrysostom* writes: "The need for sponsors became especially acute beginning with the fourth century due . . . to the fact of the sharply increased numbers of people coming to the Church. In large cities like Antioch it was simply not possible for the representatives of the Church to know the character and dispositions of the many candidates seeking Baptism, nor could they provide the individual attention necessary for a full Christian formation. Thus in addition to being a guarantor, the sponsor became a guide and teacher as well..." (pp. 54-55).

Theodore of Mopsuestia writes:

> As regards you . . . who come to Baptism, a duly appointed person inscribes your name in the Church book, together with that of your godfather, who answers for you and becomes your guide in the city and the leader of your citizenship therein. This is done in order that you may know that you are, long before the time and while still on earth, enrolled in heaven, and that your godfather who is in it has the great diligence necessary to teach you, who are a stranger and a newcomer to that great city, all the things that pertain to it and to its citizenship, so that you should be conversant with its life without any trouble and anxiety... (*Baptismal Instruction* 12, quoted in Finn, *op. cit.* p. 55).

The Greek term for sponsor αναδεχόμενος has the connotation of a "collateral" for a borrower, of "those who go surety for borrowers." St. John Chrysostom explains it to the sponsors:

> Do you wish me to address a word to those who are sponsoring you (τοὺς ἀναδεχόμενους) that they too may know what

recompense they deserve if they have shown great care for you, and what condemnation follows if they are careless? Consider, beloved, how those who go surety for someone in the matter of money are liable for it. If the borrower be well disposed, he lightens the burden of his surety; if the dispositions of his soul be ill, he makes the risk a steeper one. Wherefore the wise man counsels us saying: "if you be surety, think as if you were to pay it" (Sir. 8:13). If then those who go surety for others in the matter of money make themselves liable for the whole sum, those who go surety for others in the matter of the spirit and on an account which involves virtue should be much more alert. They ought to show their paternal love by encouraging, counseling and correcting those for whom they go surety. Let them not think that what takes place is a trifling thing, but let them see clearly that they share in the credit if by their admonition they lead those entrusted to them to the path of virtue. Again, if those they sponsor become careless, the sponsors themselves will suffer great punishment. That is why it is customary to call the sponsors "spiritual fathers," that they may learn by this very action how great an affection they must show to those they sponsor in the matter of spiritual instruction. If it is a noble thing to lead to a zeal for virtue those who are in no way related to us, much more should we fulfill this precept in the case of one whom we receive as a spiritual son. You, the sponsors, have learned that no slight danger hangs over your head if you are remiss (*Baptismal Instruction* 2, 15-16, tr. Harkins in *Ancient Christian Writers* 31, 48-49).

In commenting on this passage, Fr. Finn writes: "The sponsor's reception of the newly baptized as son clearly symbolized his obligation to see his "son's" continuing formation in Christian virtue after Baptism. Unfortunately, Chrysostom is not explicit about his duties before Baptism. However, it appears certain from the instructions that the sponsor vouched for the character, disposition, and life of the candidate at enrollment, and that sponsors and baptizands attended the instructions together. In addition, the conclusion seems inescapable that the sponsor had an important role in the moral formation of the baptizand during the catechumenate and perhaps some share in his doctrinal and liturgical instruction" (*op. cit.* p. 57).

Today the sponsors have no other functions except liturgical ones: holding the child during the rites preceeding Baptism, making answers for him, reading the Creed and receiving him from the font. The choice of sponsors has become a purely family matter and more often than not they are selected for reasons having nothing to do with the Church, her faith and the spiritual responsibility for the baptizand. And since nothing is requested from them and no one challenges them with any duties or responsibilities, the formal request that they be Orthodox sounds indeed an irrelevant one. And yet I am convinced that the institution of sponsors is needed more than ever. We no longer live in an Orthodox society and culture. And if, as a general rule, our children are still baptized, the problem of keeping them in the Church, of their religious education and upbringing, has become a truly urgent one. There is the need to "follow up" children, especially when, after having been baptized, they simply "disappear" from Church life due to their parents' indifference or neglect. There is the need for a much more systematic instruction in faith of converts to Orthodoxy. There is the need, finally, for a much closer interrelation between the educational agencies of the parish (church school, adult education, etc.) and its sacramental and liturgical life. Hence the following suggestions, which obviously ought to be discussed, studied and, if found useful and applicable, submitted to the Hierarchy for approval:

(a) That at least one of the two sponsors be appointed not by the family but by the Priest from a group of more active, concerned and educated parishioners, whose qualifications for this spiritually responsible office are to be established by the Church.

(b) That this Church-appointed sponsor be charged with "following up" the child entrusted to him by the Church and report all problems (neglect in bringing the child to the sacraments, failure to enroll him in the church school, the family's moving to another location, etc.) to the Priest.

(c) That, in addition to the usual parish records, a special book of Baptisms be kept in which the religious story of each baptized child be recorded, so that each new priest or new group of church educators is fully informed.

(d) That, in addition to a regular program of instruction for converts, one family in the parish be appointed as *sponsors* for each convert to help his integration into parish life.

The essential point in all this is that *sponsorship* is an important spiritual function within the Church and that therefore the Church, and not the family, ought to define and control it.

[5]This "Book of Life" as it is called in our present rite, or "heavenly book" (St. John Chrysostom), or "Church book" (Theodore of Mopsuestia, cf. J. Daniélou, *The Bible and the Liturgy*, pp. 19-23) is precisely the book whose reestablishment today I suggest in the previous note.

[6]Cf. Finn, *op cit.* pp. 50-51.

[7]On *Exorcisms,* cf. F. J. Dölger, "Der Exorzismus im altchristlichen Taufritual," in *Studien zum Geschichte und Kultur der Alterthum* 3, 1-2, Paderborn, 1909; H. Leclercq, "Exorcisme, éxorciste," in *Dictionnaire d'Archéologie Chrétienne et de Liturgie* 2., 2 (1910) 968-78; J. Forget, "Exorcisme, éxorciste," in *Dict. Théol. Cath.* 5. 2 (1913) 1762-86; J. Daniélou, *The Bible and the Liturgy*, pp. 23-25.

[8]*Baptismal Instructions* 2, 14. The early Church had a special ministry of exorcism not necessarily connected with priesthood. The *Apostolic Constitutions* include the following canon:

> An exorcist is not ordained. For it is a trial of voluntary goodness, and of the grace of God through Christ by the inspiration of the Holy Spirit. For he who has received the gift of healing is declared by the revelation from God, the grace which is in Him being manifest to all. But if there be occasion (for the exorcist) he must be ordained a bishop, or a presbyter, or a deacon (8, 26. Cf. *Ante-Nicene Fathers* 7, 493).

[9]Cf. St. John Chrysostom:

> Tomorrow, on Friday, at the ninth hour, you must have certain questions asked of you and you must present your contracts

(renunciation and profession) to the Master. Nor do I make mention to you of that day and that hour without some purpose. A mystical lesson can be learned from them. For on Friday at the ninth hour, the thief entered Paradise; the darkness which lasted from the sixth to the ninth hour was dissolved; and the Light, perceived by both body and mind, was taken up as a sacrifice for the whole world. For at that hour, Christ said: "Father, into your hands I commend my Spirit!" Then the sun we see looked on the Sun of Justice shining from the Cross and turned back its own rays. . . (*Baptismal Instruction* 11, 19).

Cf. also the rite of the Church of Constantinople (*Codex Barberini*) translated by Finn, *op. cit.* pp. 114-118: "the renunciation and adherence which takes place Holy Friday of the Pasch, with the archbishop presiding, and all the catechumens assembled in the very holy Church. . ." On problems connected with the time of the "renunciation" cf. Finn, *op. cit.* p. 88 ff. and Λ. Wenger, *Jean Chrysostome, Huit catechèses baptismales inédites, Sources Chrétiennes* 50, Paris, 1957, p. 80 ff.

[10]Cf. St. Cyril of Jerusalem, *Catech. Mystagog.* 1, 4:
As the West is the region of visible darkness, and since Satan, who has darkness as his lot, has his empire in the darkness, so, when you turn symbolically towards the West, you renounce this dark and obscure tyrant.
See also J. Daniélou, *The Bible and the Liturgy*, p. 27 ff.

[11]St. John Chrysostom, *Baptismal Instruction* 10, 14.

[12]*Ibid.* 10, 15.

[13]*Ibid.* 10, 15.

[14]On the "works of Satan," the *pompa diaboli*, cf. H. Rahner, "Pompa Diaboli," in *Zeitschrift für Katholische Theologie* 55 (1931) 239-73; J. Wazink, "Pompa Diaboli," in *Vigiliae Christianae* 1 (1947) 13-41; J. Daniélou, "Le démon dans la littérature ecclésiastique jusqu'a Origène," in M. Viller, *Dictionnaire de la spiritualité* 3 (1957) 151-89; M. Boismard, "I Renounce Satan, his Pomps and his Works," in *Baptism in the New Testament: A Symposium*, Baltimore, 1964, pp. 107-14.

[15]St. Cyril of Jerusalem, *Catech. mystagog.* 1, 9, trans. Cross pp. 57-58; cf. also J. Daniélou, *The Bible and the Liturgy*, p. 32, and *From Shadows to Reality*, Engl. tr. W. Hibberd, London, 1960, pp. 22-29 and 57-65.

[16]Finn, *op. cit.* p. 116.

[17]"After the contract of renunciation and attachment, after you have confessed His sovereignty, and by the words you spoke have attached yourself to Christ. . . the priest anoints you," St. John Chrysostom, *Baptismal Instruction* 2, 21. On the military oath, cf. P. Harkins in his comments to the English translation of Chrysostom's *Baptismal Instructions*, in *Ancient Christian Writers* 31, p. 214, n. 3.

[18]On the origin and the early development of the Creed see J. Kelly, *Early Christian Creeds*, ed. 2, London, 1960; also V. Neufeld, *The Earliest Christian Confessions*, Leiden, 1963; J. Jungmann, *Handing on the Faith*, Engl. tr. by A. Fuerst, ed. 2, New York, 1959.

[19]On the *redditio symboli*, cf. J. Kelly, *op cit.* pp. 32-37; Finn, *op. cit.* p. 110.

Chapter II
BAPTISM

[1]It is indeed quite typical of our present situation that while all efforts toward a more liturgical celebration of Baptism are met with suspicion if not outright opposition ("they scandalize the faithful!"), the non-compliance with even the most explicit rubrics concerning Baptism is accepted as perfectly normal. This is especially obvious with regard to this initial rubric which, as long as it is preserved in our liturgical books, shall condemn our "private" Baptisms as openly contradicting the liturgical tradition of the Church.

[2]On the religious meaning and symbolism of *water,* cf. G. van der Leeuw, *Religion in Essence and Manifestation,* Harper Torchbooks, New York 1963; M. Eliade, *The Sacred and the Profane: The Nature of Religion,* Harper Torchbooks, New York, 1961; also *Patterns in Comparative Religion,* Engl. tr. Meridian Books, Cleveland, 1963. For early Christianity, cf. H. Rahner, "The Christian Mystery and the Pagan Mysteries," in *The Mysteries, Papers from the Eranos Yearbooks* II, New York, 1955; A. D. Nock, "Hellenistic Mysteries and Christian Sacraments," in *Mnemosyne* Series 4, 5 (1952); on Christian Baptism and the use of water in the Essene Community, cf. K. Stendahl, ed., *The Scrolls and the New Testament,* New York, 1957; J. Daniélou, *Primitive Christian Symbols,* Baltimore, 1964.

[3]For a detailed study of this triple symbolism cf. Per Lundberg, *La typologie baptismale dans l'ancienne Eglise,* Uppsala, 1942; also J. Daniélou, *The Bible and the Liturgy.*

[4]On the meaning of symbolism in sacraments cf. my essay "Sacrament and Symbol," in *For the Life of the World,* St. Vladimir's Seminary Press, Crestwood, N.Y., rev. ed. 1973.

[5]The early Christian prescription is to baptize in *living water:* "Concerning Baptism, baptize thus, in the name of the Father, and of the Son and of the Holy Spirit, in living water (ἐν ὕδατι ζῶντι)" *Didache* 7, 1. This is not merely a technical term denoting running water as distinct from standing water. As O. Cullmann (*Les sacrements dans l'Évangile Johannique,* Paris, 1951, p. 22), J. Daniélou ("Living Water and the Fish," in *Primitive Christian Symbols* p. 42 ff.), and several others have shown, it carries with it extremely rich biblical references and connotations, is indeed a symbol "holding together" and revealing the cosmical, redemptive and eschatological dimensions of Baptism. Therefore not only the understanding of baptismal water as "living water" did not disappear when, at a rather early date, Baptisms began to be performed in a baptistery, but it is this understanding that determined the form and the theology of the *baptismal font,* more specifically of its octagonal shape; cf. F. J. Dölger, "Zur Symbolik des altchristlichen Taufhauses," in *Antike und Christentum* 4 (1933) 153-187. The characteristic feature of the "baptistery" was that water was carried into it by a conduit, thus remaining "living" water; cf. T. Klauser, "Taufet in libendigem Wasser," in *Pisculi,* Münster, 1969, pp. 157-60. The expression "blessing of the baptismal font" refers thus to the blessing of the baptismal water.

[6]On the origin and development of this prayer cf. H. Scheidt, "Die

Taufwasserweihegebete im Sinne vergleichender Liturgieforschung untersucht," in *Liturgiegeschichtliche Quellen und Forschungen* 29 (1935).

[7]On the *epiclesis,* the invocation of the Holy Spirit in the blessing of baptismal water, cf. J. Quasten, "The Blessing of the Baptismal Font in the Syrian Rite of the Fourth Century," in *Theological Studies* 7 (1946); also F. Cabrol, "Epiclèse," in *Dictionnaire d'Archéologie Chrétienne et de Liturgie* 5. 1, pp. 142-82, especially pp. 143-4. Cf. St. John Chrysostom: "When you come to the sacred initiation, the eyes of the flesh see water; the eyes of faith behold the Spirit," *Baptismal Instructions* 11, 12; *Ancient Christian Writers* 31, p. 164.

[8]Although the entire world has fallen under the power of the "Prince of this World," water, as the primordial element, as the "abyss," remains *the* locus and the habitation of this power. Thus water represents Death, and the Baptism of Jesus in the Jordan is the beginning of His descent into Hades, of His struggle with Death. Jordan represents all water: the purification of Jordan is a cosmical victory. On these themes in the liturgy of Epiphany cf. J. Lemarié, *La Manifestation du Seigneur, Lex Orandi* 23 Paris, 1957, p. 305 ff. Also J. Daniélou, *The Bible and the Liturgy,* and P. Lundberg, *op. cit.* p. 10 ff.

[9]On the meaning and uses of *oil* in the ancient world cf. A. S. Pease, "Oleum," in Pauly-Wissowa, *Real Encyclopedie der Classischen Altertumswissenschaft;* for Old Testament cf. A.R.S. Kennedy, "Anointing," in Hasting's *Dictionary of the Bible,* New York, 1909, p. 35; L. L. Mitchell, *Baptismal Anointing,* London, 1966.

[10]The meaning of this pre-baptismal anointment as *recreation* of man through forgiveness of sins and healing is beautifully expressed in the prayer of Bishop Serapion of Thmuis (fourth century), a prayer in regard to the anointing with oil of those who are being baptized:

> Master, lover of men and lover of souls, compassionate and pitiful, O God of truth, we invoke Thee following out and obeying the promises of Thine Only-Begotten who has said: "whosesoever sins you forgive, they are forgiven them" (St. John 20: 23): and we anoint with this anointing oil those who in purpose approach this divine regeneration, beseeching Thee that our Lord Jesus Christ may work in them healing and strength-making power, and by this anointing oil may reveal Himself and heal away from their soul, body, and spirit every mark of sin and lawlessness or satanic fault, and by His own proper grace may afford them remission, that dying to sin they shall live in righteousness, and *being recreated through this anointing,* and being cleansed through the washing, and being renewed in the Spirit, they shall be able henceforth to have victory over all the opposing energies and deceits of this world that assail them, and thus to be bound up and united with the flock of our Lord and Savior Jesus Christ... (John Wordsworth, *Bishop Serapion's Prayer Book,* pp. 74-76).

As we shall see later in this essay the exact significance of this pre-baptismal anointment became the object of a heated controversy among several Western theologians mainly because of the absence of references to any post-baptismal anointment (*Chrismation* or *Confirmation*) in the ancient Syrian tradition: Chrysostom (cf. Finn, *op. cit.,* p. 139 ff), the *Didascalia*

Apostolorum and the *Liturgical Homilies of Narsai* (cf. R. Connolly, *Didascalia Apostolorum*, pp. 48-50; *ibid. Lit. Hom. of Narsai*, pp. 42-49) as well as in other documents (cf. H. Green, "The Significance of the Pre-Baptismal Seal in St. John Chrysostom," in *Studia Patristica* 6. 6 [1962] pp. 84-90). This in turn led to a debate on confirmation in its relationship to Baptism. Personally I am convinced that this debate was due to false presuppositions proper to the Western approach to sacraments in general, and to Baptism in particular. The entire baptismal mystery is in the Spirit and by the Spirit, so that at each of its three stages—pre-baptismal anointment, Baptism and Chrismation—it is the Holy Spirit who acts and fulfills this rite. It is the man recreated by the Holy Spirit (pre-baptismal anointment) who dies with Christ in the baptismal font and is regenerated by the Holy Spirit (Baptism) so that he may receive the Holy Spirit Himself as new and immortal life in the Kingdom of God (Chrismation). One act, one gift posits the next one and is fulfilled in it so that only in its total "ordo" is the whole meaning of the liturgy revealed.

[11]On Baptism in the academic theology of the nineteenth century, cf. F. Gavin, *Some Aspects of Contemporary Greek Orthodox Thought*, pp. 306-316; Bp. Sylvester, *Opyt Pravoslavnogo Dogmaticheskogo Bogosloviia* (*Orthodox Dogmatic Theology*) vol. 4, ed. 2, pp. 422-425.

[12]On these controversies see A. Almazov, *Istoriia*, p. 283 ff.; Trembelas, vol. 3, pp. 99 ff.

[13]For Trembelas, for example, only sacraments are "means of grace": "Without ignoring the power and the necessity of prayer and preaching of the word of God, we do not list them among the specific means which confer grace: only divinely instituted sacraments are such means..." (*op. cit.* p. 9); cf. also Gavin, *op. cit.* p. 272 ff.

[14]On the use of this psalm cf. Almazov, *Istoriia*, pp. 426-427.

CHAPTER III
THE SACRAMENT OF THE HOLY SPIRIT

[1]Λαμπρὸν τὸ ἔσθημα, Wenger, *Sources Chrétiennes*, 101.

[2]St. John Chrysostom, *Baptismal Instruction* 2, 25; Wenger, *Sources Chrétiennes*, 50, p. 147.

[3]*Ibid.* 8, 25.

[4]Cf. Almazov, *Istoriia*, p. 430 ff.; Finn, *op. cit.* p. 191 ff.; Daniélou, *Bible and Liturgy*, chap. 2; cf. also E. Peterson, "Religion et vêtement," in *Rythmes du monde*, 1946, and *Pour une théologie du vêtement*, Lyon, 1943.

[5]Peterson, "Religion et vêtement," p. 4.

[6]St. Ambrose, *De Myst.* 34. Cf. also St. Gregory of Nyssa, in Hamman, *Baptism*, p. 122 ff.

[7]For the history of these controversies cf. B. Neunheuser, *Baptism and Confirmation*, tr. J. Hughes, The Herder History of Dogma, New York, 1964.

J. Crehan, S. J., "Ten Years' Work on Baptism and Confirmation: 1945-1955," in *Theological Studies* 17 (1956) 494-516.

[8]B. Neunheuser, chap. 11.

[9]B. Neunheuser, chap. 10.

[10]Bp. Sylvester, *op. cit.*, p. 425 ff. Cf. also Gavin, *op. cit.*, p. 316, ff.; Trembelas, *op. cit.*, p. 132.

[11]*Ibid.* and also Gavin, p. 317 ff.

[12]On *gift* (δωρεά) of F. Büchsel, article "δίδωμι, δῶρον... δωρεά etc." in G. Kittel, *Theol. Dict. of the New Testament,* vol. 2, pp. 166 ff. On *gifts* as χαρίσματα, cf. H. Conzelmann, article "χάρισμα, χαρίσματα," in G. Friedrich, *Theol. Dict. of the New Testament,* vol. 9, pp. 402 ff.

[13]Cf. F. J. Dölger, *Sphragis,* Paderborn, 1911. Also Daniélou, *Bible and Liturgy,* chap. 3; J. Ysebaert, *Greek Baptismal Terminology: Its Origin and Early Development,* Nijmegen (1962); A. Stenzel, *Die Taufe. Eine generische Erklärung der Taufliturgie,* Innsbruck, 1957.

[14]*In II. Corinth.* Hom. 3, 4; *Patr. Graeca* 41, 411.

[15]On the religious origin and connotations of kingship cf. G. van der Leeuw, *Religion in its Essence and Manifestations,* vol. 1, p. 13.

[16]Cf. Paul Daubin, S. J., *Le Sacerdoce Royal des Fidèles dans la tradition ancienne et moderne,* Paris, 1950.

Chapter IV
THE ENTRANCE INTO THE KINGDOM

[1]On the *baptisterion,* its meaning and function in the baptismal liturgy, cf. F. J. Dölger, "Zur Symbolik des altchristlichen Taufhauses: Das Oktagon und die Symbolik der Achtzahl," in *Antike und Christenthum* 4 (1943) pp. 153-87. H. Leclercq, "Baptistère," in *Dictionnaire d'Archéologie Chrétienne et de Liturgie* 2. 1, 382-469. W. M. Bedard, *Symbolism of the Baptismal Font,* Washington, 1951.

[2]On the post-baptismal procession cf. St. Ambrose, *De Myst.* 43; St. Gregory of Nazianzen, *Patr. Graeca* 36, 425 A; Daniélou, *Bible and Liturgy.*

[3]I shall discuss the pre-entrance part of the Divine Liturgy in my forthcoming book on the Eucharist. Cf. my article "Tainstvo Vkhoda" ("The Mystery of the Entrance") in *Vestnik Russkogo Studencheskogo Khristianskogo Dvizheniia* (Messenger of the Russian Student Christian Movement) 111 (Paris, 1974).

[4]In fact there exists no comprehensive study of the double eucharistic celebration at Easter. The same development took place in the West: cf. J. W. Tyrer, *Historical Survey of Holy Week, Its Services and Ceremonial,* Alcuin Club Collections 29, London, 1932, p. 169 ff. As to the East, liturgiologists seem to ignore it as a problem: cf. Lazar Mirkovich's *Kheortologiia* (*Heortology*), in Serbian, Belgrade, 1961, p. 62 ff. The major difficulty is that all existing *Typika* are posterior to the development of that practice.

Cf. A. Dimitrievsky, *Opisanie liturgicheskikh rukopisei* (*Description of Liturgical Manuscripts*) vol. 1. *Typika*, Kiev 1895. Cf. also his *Bogosluzhenie strastnoi i paskhalnoi sedmits vo sv. Ierusalime* (*The liturgy of the Holy and Paschal Weeks in Jerusalem in ninth-tenth centuries*) Kazan, 1894; G. Orlov, *Ob"iasnenie paskhalnogo bogosluzheniia* (*Explanation of Paschal Liturgy*) Moscow, 1898. It seems likely that the double celebration of the paschal Eucharist—mentioned already in Etheria's *Peregrinatio* 38—originated in Jerusalem. I hope to deal with this problem in a special study, *Pascha and Pentecost.*

[5]Cf. St. John Chrysostom: "...As soon as they come up from the waters they are led to the awesome table heavy laden with countless favors, where they taste of the Master's Body and Blood, and become a dwelling place for the Holy Spirit" (*Baptismal Instructions* 2, 27; tr. Harkins, in *Ancient Christian Writers* 31, p. 53). A general study of that "interdependence" is provided in Daniélou's *Bible and Liturgy,* chaps. 9-10; cf. also Almazov, *Istoriia,* p. 438. It was still self-evident to Symeon of Thessalonica (fifteenth century) who writes: "This constitutes the fulfillment of all sacraments that, being free from sinful uncleanness, and having become pure and sealed to Christ in the Holy Spirit, we would partake of the Body and Blood of Christ Himself and would be bodily united to Him" (*Pisaniia Sv. Ottsov: Uchitelei Tserkvi,* vol. 2, St. Petersburg, 1856, p. 73, in Russian). The manuals of dogmatics, however, simply ignore all this (cf. Sylvester, *op. cit.,* p. 455 ff.; Gavin, *op. cit.,* p. 316 ff.; Trembelas, *op. cit.,* p. 139 ff.).

[6]On the *rites of the eighth day* cf. Almazov, *Istoriia,* pp. 466-475; Symeon of Thessalonica, *op. cit.,* pp. 74-75; F. Cabrol, "La Semaine Sainte et les origines de l'Année Liturgique," in *Les Origines Liturgiques,* Paris, 1906.

[7]On the Eighth Day in Christian theology and spirituality cf. *Le Jour du Seigneur* (a collection of essays) Paris, 1948, and Daniélou, *Bible and Liturgy,* chap. 16: "The Eighth Day."

[8]"Thou art *justified,* thou art *illumined,* thou art *sanctified,* thou art *washed...*" "Here," writes Bishop Benjamin, "all words, with the exception of the last one ('washed') refer to the three sacraments fulfilled in the neophyte. 'Justified' indicates that his sins were forgiven... 'Illumined' refers to Baptism... 'Chrismated' to Chrismation. And 'sanctified' to Holy Communion" (*Novaia Skrizhal',* ed. 14, St. Petersburg, 1844, p. 364, in Russian).

[9]On *tonsure* cf. van der Leeuw, *Religion,* p. 42-3; Almazov, *op. cit.,* p. 445 ff.

Chapter V
THE CHURCHING

[1]For general religious background of these rites cf. M. Eliade, *The Sacred and the Profane,* New York, 1959, especially chap. 4: "Human Existence and Sanctified Life," p. 162 ff. Also by him, *Rites and Symbols of Initiation,* New York, 1958. Van der Leeuw, *Religion,* section 22: "The Sacred Life," and section 49: "Purification." On the rite cf. Almazov, *Istoriia,* p. 476 ff.

[2]On the religious meaning of names cf. H. Usener, *Gotternamen,* 1929; Van der Leeuw, *Religion,* section 17.

CONCLUSION

[1]The main question here is, of course, that of re-establishing the liturgical and, therefore, spiritual link between Baptism and the Eucharist, the sacrament of the entrance into the Church and the Sacrament of the Church. In the past, and even after the connection of Baptism with Pascha (or the other "baptismal feasts": Christmas, Epiphany and Lazarus Saturday) was broken, the practice was to give Communion to the newly baptized with the non-consumed Holy Gifts. This indicates that Baptism was performed immediately after the Liturgy (cf. Symeon of Thessalonica, *op. cit.,* pp. 73 ff.). This practice is still common among the Greeks. But although this practice is obviously better than the total disconnection of Baptism from the Eucharist, it is still a deficient one: we have said enough I hope to show how not only Communion, but the entire Eucharist truly is the fulfillment of the baptismal mystery.

The only adequate solution consists therefore in reinstating *baptismal liturgies,* i.e. the celebration of Baptism before the Divine Liturgy yet in organic liturgical connection with it. How to achieve this must be the object of careful study, discussion and ultimately approval by the hierarchy, without whose sanction, permission and blessing, nothing ought to be done in the Church. Therefore the following suggestions are made tentatively, as a starting point of a much needed liturgical and pastoral discussion.

A. It seems proper that the pre-baptismal part of our present liturgy of initiation, i.e. the *Prayers at the Reception of the Catechumens,* including Exorcisms, the Renunciation of Satan, the Conversion to Christ, and the Confession of Faith, rites which as we know took place either during the entire period of the catechumenate, or in a service distinct from Baptism proper, be performed *before* the Liturgy. Thus, for example, if the Divine Liturgy is to begin at 10:00 A.M., the pre-baptismal rites can be scheduled for 9:30 A.M. The place for these rites is the "vestibule."

B. I suggest that when preceeded by Baptism, the opening Doxology, "Blessed is the Kingdom..." should be made by the celebrant as he stands at the baptismal font and should be followed immediately by the Great Litany, with the inclusion in it of the petitions for the blessing of the water.

C. The baptismal rites are then performed: the Blessing of Water, the anointment of the water and the baptizand with the oil of gladness, the baptismal immersion, the rite of the white garment and the Chrismation.

D. Immediately after Chrismation, the celebrant leads the newly baptized in the circular procession around the font, while the congregation sings "As many as have been baptized..." and, after the third circle, leads them to the steps of the ambo where they will remain with their sponsors until Communion. The choir: "Glory. . . Have put on Christ. . ." And then the final "As many. . ." during which the celebrant enters the Altar, kisses the Holy Table and proceeds to the High Place.

E.   Two prokeimena: of Baptism and of the day; two Gospel readings: of Baptism and of the day.

F.   Then, the Liturgy continues as usual. To mark the particularity of this celebration, the litanies and prayers for the catechumens may be omitted.

G.   The newly baptized shall receive Communion before all other communicants.

H.   The post-baptismal rites, if for the sake of convenience they are to take place on the same day, are performed after the *Dismissal*.

On which *days* should baptismal liturgies be celebrated? Sunday may present some practical difficulties. Therefore, by analogy with Easter, the best day in my opinion is *Saturday*. The day should be announced to the entire parish, so that as many of its members as possible can attend the mystery of new birth and take part in it.

It must be clear, however, that such liturgical restoration would bear no fruits unless it is properly prepared by appropriate teaching and preaching, i.e. by the deepening of the Church's mind. The liturgy must *reveal* the Church's faith, make it a living one. Thus no liturgical changes will fulfill anything if they are not the expression and the fulfillment of our own reconversion to the true meaning and power of our Orthodox faith.